SELECTED POEMS

John Ash

SELECTED POEMS

CARCANET

First published in 1996 by
Carcanet Press Limited
402-406 Corn Exchange Buildings
Manchester M4 3BY

A CIP catalogue record for this book
is available from the British Library
ISBN 1 85754 155 3

The publisher acknowledges financial assistance
from the Arts Council of England

Set in 10 pt Garamond Simoncini by Bryan Williamson, Frome
Printed and bound in England by SRP Ltd, Exeter

Contents

Part One: Manchester

Part Two: New York

Part One: Manchester

from **The Bed**

Even though

the suspension bridges are buckling in the hurricane
and several cars full of conventional families
with an average number of children have been thrown
into a river full of alligators,

the old house is still there in its 'extensive grounds'
its doorways linking the clauses of rooms and corridors
into a majestic sentence that will not reveal its object

      (it might be only a patch of unusual colour
or a child's excited view through a bedroom keyhole)

the windows open onto the white of the margin
rainclouds are a shop girl's dusty thumb-prints

                          a word
is a hand a throat a strand of hair damp after an evening's dancing

the branching stairs escape syntax –
are the extreme point of muscular tension translated into stone

you collapse sprawling across the marble prefix as

the first door opens with a hollow sound out of a cheap horror movie
shown late on friday when we are a little stoned or drunk
and very easily frightened

                 A cat escapes into the garden
and a rich dust rises in welcome. Oh! the fineness of the objects!
their colours! Garbo's hat with the feather in it, the heaps
of early sixties singles, the Afghan gloves, the burnished globes,
the toy trains, the mouldy jellies and rose-coloured maps of empire!

It is all perfect: the mirrors are hardly tarnished at all
and still flicker with the faces of unhappy children.

We have stepped into the frontispiece of a new book:
it is called 'The History of Pleasure'.

Starting from Clouds

In what sense can they be said to 'gather' –
isn't it more a question of them advancing
over the landscape, ironing-out differences in the light?

They ought to resemble a very grandiose
kind of public building –
Piranesian, for example:
the Palais de Justice, Bruxelles.

*

A munitions factory in the rain
jets of steam rising from the steel plant
visible beyond the contaminated marsh

a din of sirens:
civilians are being evacuated –
say, 60,000 of them
in a calm orchestrated manner.

The sky is clear –
for the moment.

*

A landscape of broken dice, ice-floes...
the city is being carried away by its river.

From the tower of the Exhibition Centre
the coin-operated telescope
reveals a scene of square-jawed actors
conversing with exiled dictators.

Diamonds and blue-prints spill
from instrument cases: the whole
is subject to a rigid geometry.

*

The hospital for tropical diseases
is closed by strikes. A gull dips
at the splash of a gun dropped in the river.

*

The clouds mass into the fierce head
of a political theorist above the cold bay water

from the shape of their mouths
we know the drowned negroes have raised their voices.

*

The tourists are astonished to find themselves
standing on the open hand of liberty
as the rain slants in towards them

from the empty houses and the snarled highway,
the bridge that might as well be inverted
for the good it does: the irises

of their camera shutters
open.

*

                        from the classical
façade of the disused factory
issues a nauseating, sweetish

smell: the dead cannot be buried here
and a hedge of barbed-wire surrounds them.

It is a place where once the taxi-driver
has dropped you
he will not wait.

Early Views of Manchester and Paris: First View

It makes us uncomfortable: the pillars
and shadowed arches of these monuments
to commerce are a furniture we can't
or daren't throw out. Hard not to admire
such a total dedication to redundancy, –

as if the whole city were a railway station
and the line diverted. In the photographs
of that age the only people to be visible
were those who stood for long periods
without moving. Only when it began
to die did the running mob appear
as dim smudges on a bridge in Paris.

And now are they visible?
Do they move freely?

Processional I

There has been disease in the white town
among the rocks and trees. The masks
of its theatre

look towards it with stopped howls
and grimaces. A procession emerges
from a black, unguarded gate

crossing the bridge over the ravine
moving towards tombs on its far side.
The soldiers wear

helmets like broken cages.
Their distorted armour suggests wings
or extraneous limbs.

Their heads are beaked and sharp
or fissured stones, without profile, –
the divine monsters

of Karnak turned decrepit. There seems
no reason why this parade should end.
It could

repeat and repeat. But the men
and the soldiers were not always like these
who carry the dead

on makeshift litters trailing rags
to the tombs on the far side
of the long bridge.

And the tombs cut from the rock –
their façades represent houses, villas and farms,
amiable gods and domestic scenes.

Two men with crimped beards lean on their staffs,
play dice on a mosaiced floor; a child
rolls a hoop

before a hedge of roses and a dog curls
asleep on a step. Two women
bid each other farewell, –

their hands are touching, – the narrow
folds of their shifts fall from their shoulders
to their feet.

The figures show traces of vivid earth-reds
and lapis blues. The stone flames
and it is already evening.

The procession is still crossing the bridge.
Over bearers and corpses is the patina
of exhausted metals.

The Last Photographs

The full colour photographs
of the 'innocent victims'

were to be buried in the usual way
under a mountain of flowers

transported by air from hot-
houses half a world away:

the fact that it had been intended
to build a 'utopia' on their deaths

made no difference to them –
'no appreciable difference'.

Words were said to the water
which fell from a sprinkler on

to identical wooden lids.

A few days later, the sewage farm
exploded with catastrophic results.

Nothing could be done about it.
The police and the fire service were trapped

behind enormous metal shutters
which refused to operate.

The desolation became general
and daily more picturesque.

In the last photograph to be taken
before the entire area was sealed

off, a black flock of birds descends
towards the snow-bound city –

descends in the shape of a neckline,
descends like a frustrated wish.

Prose for Roy Fisher

The mud dries out. The new reservoir has covered everything, – even
the big house. Also the telephone kiosk, the greenhouses and the cat's
grave with its plastic flowers.

It was necessary. The towns have to drink, – water, the past. They can't
choose what they drink or how much: they swell up and burst over the
landscape.

The cat screams and hisses in the pipes all night. The big house rises
shimmering on television screens: even on colour sets it is a blinding
white, inhabited by bored actors. Everyone mistakes the water-weeds
for ivy. The plastic flowers

get more approximate: they're not even symbols anymore, only a
drained colour. And heavy sleepers wake to find tumblers emptied of
water, marked by someone's lips: not theirs, not theirs…

(It is at the moment of surfacing from sleep
we know we have drowned. And it happened years ago.)

   blue shadows in white sheets. The dawn

is a denial repeated so many times no-one can remember the object of
the denial. It stretches the point. (I don't want to know this: no one
does.) It is reflected in a lake shaped like someone asleep on his side,
and not dreaming. Along the shores the mud dries out and cracks: a
glaze badly fired.

Landscape and Figures

Exploded geography!

Are we lost with no better equipment
than a broken thermometer, no
entertainment other than
the endless discussion of 'relationships'?
This isn't the place we planned
to arrive at...

Mountains shiver at a touch. The waves
of the lake are too small or too large
for the surrounding indigo forest;
its sailing boats have only one side
held out towards the camera
by embarrassed children.

Sounds follow the colours:
klangfarbenmelodie
– coming towards us, confused whispers
of an unspecified anguish which
the distance makes musical.

Whose are the voices? What laws
govern us here? Even
if the compass hadn't fallen
into a crevice of the glacier
it would've been useless, since
everything is faintly magnetised,
faintly glistening... So –

start with the establishment
of principles: analysis
of tonal systems.

Sonata in Two Sentences

It is centuries since hunting horns sounded here
and only literature makes us imagine them
like the dead roses that meant so much to the young
cavalry officer toying with an elegant pistol at his temple

in blue mists under a moon that really is
a coin thrown for a wager, stuck

at the height of its trajectory. Since we conceive
even the sexual parts as metaphors this
late air or last song is carried easily beyond

the matter of trees reddening or moths
dying at our windows, and something more final
which may not return goes up in smoke
from gardens, fumes from industrial estates

to orchestrate unrecognisably
the plain sonata of a sun descending.

Some Boys (or The English Poem circa 1978)

It's like sorting through fireworks
left out all night in the damp garden –
the same acrid smell, the same
refusal to ignite. The world appears
as a very dull novel in which the characters –
Edwin, Wanda, Septimus and Moira,
are constantly looking out of windows to observe,
bleakly or with sighs, that it is raining again.

Who'd believe that gods could appear in the shadows
of this street, helmetted, surrounded by
blue clouds? Only some boys
gunning the motors of their stationary bikes –

but they have nowhere to go
and don't want to be written about.

Their myth is violent and orderly. Friends!
a word, a clear word on the death of culture,
the cognac-coloured sunset darkening above
the hunched shoulders of house-roofs, the lilacs or...

the tangled mess of crashed motorbikes
and choruses of weeping girls from soap-operas!

Orchestral Manoeuvres (In the Dark)

We're working forward from Bach, –
Bach The Father,
but we seem to have got stuck round about Brahms.

Most symphonies occur every two or three years.
We aren't interested in the unimportant rhapsodies

or nocturnes. It is night now, –
a winter's night as it happens

and we've left the town outside,
steaming in the cold...

The recital of nostalgias begins. The soprano
seems to be using up all the available air, –

colour drains from the flowers at the edge of the stage,
the lights grow dim (alternatively
they grow intolerably bright). Up there

an invisible child is taking
a long time to die, –

and it needn't happen!
the miracle cure was discovered
half a century ago. But how

irrelevant this is! It is the privilege
of 'art' as we understand it, to ignore
these developments

            and somehow the town
outside and the century it is currently lodged in –
one step on its pitiless journey
to a lower destination than it thinks
it deserves – doesn't seem to have much talent

for expressing itself in those long loops of sound
we like to think of as 'immortal melodies', –
the phrases, the links emerge unevenly, clank and fall apart.

So when the orchestra arrives
at Vienna circa 1909 it turns back –

Farewell Gustav, great Arnold
Anton and Alban!...

The orchestra is a kind of vehicle rolling
back and forth across two centuries
flattening Alps for our convenience.

Advanced Choreography for Beginners

They are trying to waltz to the drum solo
when the American football-player crashes into the band-stand

O anger and incomprehension! he is chased away, down
the green alleys of a park, the footfalls muffled by thick moss

All at once it gets foggy and very still: the angel crosses the stage
smoking a cigar, the mechanical wings flapping slowly

then, in the nick of time the violin resumes before the rose can fade
or the stars fall out of the polished arc of heaven

Suddenly! the footwear cascades onto the stage:
so much of it, –
boots, clogs, sandals, sneakers, espadrilles

in the final scene a lot of people are smoking wooden pipes
decorated with shredded paper beards

a woman carries a table-lamp across the stage for no reason
(and this, presumably, is the point of it) there are

piles of polystyrene chips there is a fan-dance
and a mad man

the point is:

to establish a new lyricism in which all these things will find their place
equally like buildings on the loop of a promenade
doors and windows open towards a calm sea that reminds us
inevitably of a sheet of cellophane that has been crumpled up
and smoothed out again, but not completely –

Salon Pieces

Instead of the Chinese lanterns
think of the 'beautiful sorrows'
cultivated in the idleness of a lost age –
a riding whip lying across an open book,
the immense trees of the park
shuddering after the rainstorm –

yes, the world is simple
and very far from our lives

      *

I like this picture
even if its charm is suspect

You can almost smell the lavender water
The word 'Proustian' comes to mind...
(Why, I wonder? It could be the wallpaper –
the motif of a church spire emerging
from trees echoing the 'real' spire,
and the 'real' trees glimpsed through the window.)

      *

Again, the alcoholic symphony. But which part?
Is this development or recapitulation?
It seems important to know: pleasure's not simple.

No doubt something will supersede 'opium
and the shameful vices', but so far
moving pictures have not been invented.
The lithe young heroine whose eyes *shine*
with the hope of the world has not arrived
to enliven the upholstery and the drapes.

The dream of empire continues. Only
the green dome of the Opera
is visible above the rain-forest.

Beware of gorillas, stone-fish etc...

The nightmares are boring
and will not go away

(a motto theme by César Franck)

The Rain

'Not a storm, but the world cried that day…'
                                    – Sonny Stitt
        for Roy Edwards

There may be a heaven of musicians
or an angel who weeps for us
but the question doesn't need to be answered, –

the simple grandeur of the 'correspondence'
submerges the inadequate, solo response
which is now a broken-down pram or birdcage
at the bottom of a Lake of Tears
that shines and shines with a more than natural clarity
        we haven't had to manufacture –
polishing up old feelings
like fifth-century coins retrieved from the midden,
remembering stone wings rain-eaten in cemeteries by canals
and this was what we wanted,
something that would throw a cool light, stopping short
of indifference, onto the tragically altered landscape
revealed with the abruptness of a stage-set, –
the empty chairs, cushions and useless reading lamps (it's clear
this story will never be told: the hired costumes
are returned to the agency) and we won't need to ask
questions about the flowers, their colours or number,
their aptness for the awful occasion:
it will now be possible to describe this new and too familiar
sense of loss with some appearance of calm –

'not that it happened so far away I didn't hear about it
just far enough for my feelings in the matter to be redundant
although in the next street where the evening shower had started
in the next room, the one where the radio had been turned off

interrupting the song
about the lemon trees in bloom'

The event is obscured
in the hoot and hiss of cars returning
to elegant districts indifferently embroidering the outskirts of the town
and it will be lost –
for a song is too obvious, sticking like a motto
and neither your life nor mine resembles one,
but the longing stays with us –

I mean the golden longing

the idea revolved in sleep of another land
where the people find 'anxiety' no more than amusing or exotic
where the rain is music on the roofs of blue-shuttered towns
springing perfumes out of dusty yards. Oh, do you know?
the life there moves in loops and circles so wide
that not a single child is sick into the flower-beds
and each evening above the domes and bar-signs there is
harmless lightning in a mauve and pink sky: it is
a masterpiece by some great anonymous mannerist,
reproduced again and again without loss, –
yours forever, to sleep with. And a song is the engine
that builds this different climate, taking from both spring and autumn
buds, leaves, and fruit but avoiding
absolutes; its disorder is so strangely calm
that soon each phenomenon encountered
seems an obedient medium, answering your desires
even when unknown (closed in a monastic crypt
of your own making, painted with mediaeval depictions
of 'the tortures of conscience'). The world attends the song:
the daughters of music stand like pillars on either side an open doorway
welcoming the handsome guests, and just to know
the invitations have somehow arrived and are answered
in this shirtless and laughing style
redeems all the waiting through blank uncounted years

that are now caught like a distant line of poplars in the backward flood
        of light, –
characters in the exquisite fable that was always there
on the big table by the window but unread until this moment.

Omissions in the intimate journals
deepen to flower-filled canyons
and the winding descent is an act of great impersonal tenderness
rewarded by the sound of a river moving quickly far below us –
where it comes from or is going we don't know:
the rumour of lakes and populous deltas is enough.

                *

We have to love the past
it is our invention. Perhaps, after all
forgiveness is the proper attitude
and we should not abolish history but make a space in it
that will contain both the philosophies
of eighteenth-century boudoirs and the Kingdom of Meroe,
the Empire of Songhoi… and the place
where the last Carib leapt to his death
and the place where the last prince of the Palaeologi
is buried are the same in our understanding:
the sky is the same and the sea. So
the primitive thumb-piano hacked from the edge
of your mother's kitchen table can now encompass
all the masterpieces of our literature, –
the great fugues, consumptive nocturnes and love elegies…
It is right that we don't know what to expect, –
this revival of polyphony could alter entirely
the simple relation of sound to colour, or sharpen
to the fineness of a stylus our dulled anticipation
of the storm that still holds off, –
flickering and crashing in some closed department of time
like a shoe shifting in its box, already entered
by the idea of the foot. We don't forget
that the light comes from inside, is an oblong of limited extent
with thickets bristling at its edges, but are still moved
by the idea of creatures and places that do not exist
and are necessary: we don't believe in them
but this rain is weeping nonetheless and the flowers grief, –

the wilted petals are the colour of hospital corridors, but the scent, –
the scent of the flowers is like a murmurous greeting
in a language you do not understand, in the bald dictionary
        sense of understanding,
but its mere sound creates fresh sentiments, lithe figures
for the alcoves prepared long in advance, capped by the shell of desire.

The Northern Symphonies

The pines shiver expecting winter
vanishing in mist

moths circle the lights of railway platforms
at intervals through a thousand, two thousand miles

The peasants are painting dolls –
dolls within dolls

the children of aristocrats
are collecting mushrooms and butterflies

the river erases all the names
of adolescents written out in the sand

and their letters remain undiscovered
as the wooden bridges split slowly apart

The empty palace is painted green and gold
snow has fallen in the square

a crowd brings down the statue at its centre
soon no-one can remember

whether it represented
a man or a woman

O how cold the air is!
what bitter tiredness

and how unexpectedly sad
the faces of the crowd...

There is a loud cracking sound
as if a great river suddenly thawed
as if a ship fired all its guns at once

an enormous mirror stands up
and in an instant dissolves
running in all directions like spilt mercury

melting snow washes blood from the birch copse –
how will the new life begin?

Accompaniment to a Film Scene

Start with the knowledge
that representation is not enough,
that the aim is –

a 'sense of reality' that deepens
when realism is abandoned,

when the sea at night is sheets
of gleaming black plastic lashed into a storm
by men concealed under them with long poles,
when the love-scene takes place in a conical room
decorated with Japanese erotica

                        and, yes, of course
there are two or more people doing something on the bed –
just as, on occasion, real spray hits the painted backdrop;
there are also soft moans and sighs that penetrate
the hubbub of the score to fill us
with a destructive nostalgia that confuses everything, –

the views of various cities
gardens and coastlines –

trees breaking into red flower
at the wrong season...

But there is no sense of guilt:
this is no deception but a form of imitation
unconnected to ordinary ideas
of accuracy. Buildings and mountains
are reproduced exactly, but all much larger
than life size. It is the details of the small things
time abolished in the person of an efficient
waiter wiping the table clean are more difficult
to establish. Were there crayfish
and burst figs? Ashtrays and paper napkins?

It's certain the sauces were much too rich
but the profound words spoken in our cups
have proved no more durable than sky-writing
announcing a forthcoming boatshow or rodeo,

and it is increasingly difficult to disguise the general air
of 'nervousness bordering on panic'. The project
has already exceeded by millions the estimated
budget, and problems remain: it isn't enough
just to paint the skies, clouds must be seen to move
and we are experimenting urgently with several
different kinds of vapour jet. There's still the fear
that we'll arrive one day to find the gates of the dream-
studio closed behind a huge cocaine-white disc
on which the words NO ENTRY are written in blood,
and the backers withdrawn to penthouses on private
asteroids, from which they send us letters
demanding repossession, concluding in signatures
of a fantastic and lethal elegance.

Glowing Embers: Paraphrases & Fictions

for Blaise Cendrars

The idea was to be at the centre of things, –
but where was the centre?

I moved around a lot
and this from an early age, –

from the time
my father locked me in the shed with the cattle
because I wouldn't listen
to the clockmaker or the priest, –
so what? I didn't like their smell...

Mother cried often
grandfather lived only
for the strawberries he planted each year
our house stood on the summit of a cliff

at the foot of which the narrow track of a railway
curved rapidly out of sight to east and west
beyond that lay the town – old and famous for its beauty –
which I despised: I escaped

and ran over some mountains –
they cannot have been so high
it is only now that the light reflected from their snows

is dazzling...

The sense of freedom was so vast that stars seemed grains of sugar
dissolving on my tongue
at last I fell asleep surrounded by herbs
on the platform of a deserted station

I woke to the smell of a rich tobacco
a Russian liked the look of me
(he didn't ask much)
and the revolution of 1917
was one of many events that I witnessed

I fell in love with the swimming pools and dancebands of ocean-going
     liners
(once I danced on the deck at night with a little mulatto wet-nurse
while in the stern emigrants from Galicia sang savagely of old revolts
and phosphorescence glittered in the wake)

I became familiar with mountains with indelicate names
'Fossil Claw' 'Mother's Belly' 'Lion's Rump'

The English were atrocious
the odour of their cabbage followed me for months
the French threw me out
and the Germans, – the Germans
the only one whose company I could endure
was the young soldier whose corpse I found frozen one winter
high in the Jura mountains

but I embraced the violent innocence
I found in America's great heart

I loved the rigidity of modern hotels, the metallic chatter of radio
     advertisements
the music of jukeboxes and discothèques
and equally
the grace of colonial mansions covered with moss beside rivers so wide
     their far banks were invisible
Chopin sonatas

I loved equally the women of Rio and the young men of Manila
I observed the dawn in the straits of Molucca
before the bridges of San Francisco, the towers of New York
and amid the small islands of the Aegean, scattered like pumice

I travelled I regained my religious faith and lost it
I lived for months on a diet of oranges and water

it may be that in the shadows of some dismal port
reeking of oil and fish and urine
I once killed a man, –
and yes it must be so, for the odours of the place stand up like statues
     staring at me in horror

Who was the woman with red hair
I loved in the Levant?
She astonished the merchants of Saturday morning with her evening
    dress and naked feet, –
also I remember a balcony a bed the sound of rain on dry leaves in
    autumn
all imprinted with that name now illegible to me

At last I forgot my mother At last I forgot my home, –
only a faint bitterness remained, a faint sweetness

a thimble of salt a dish of strawberries...

I was nostalgic for all places and all times
and I was eager to push forward

my every action cast the shadow which is contemplation –

and I sang

Severe Concepts

That was dangerous –
sighing for a hat.

Who pulls on gloves
before starting this work

few will pay for? The black
implement is regressing
to its place in a swan's wing

and the lines are blue as
aristocratic blood. The effect

is Japanese: apple blossom
swelling to the horizon, on and on, –

and the man who has denied
the world still labours

under the weight of the great bronze
bowl which contains.... Well

what *does* it contain? Can it be eaten?
Will it keep us warm? Will it

help us to reach the hostel on the
far side of the hill, –
putting energy into the legs?

And what does the inscription say?
Along the rim the severe
concepts are worn to a ghostly

lustre. You can't fit 'love'
into the structure you imagined
and even the most common objects, –

the cracked cup, the armchair
stand off at some distance

shrouded in a spurious
mystery, refusing

to come in as if they wanted
to be part of some very
picturesque mythology for which

you patently don't possess the key.
But, what will occupy
the deserted space, since

forest and absolute night hold off?
The sadness like a courtyard

surrounding the statement
of a vow that will be broken.

The Bed

'...O, wie alt ist unser Geschlecht
Jemand flüstert drunten im Garten; jemand hat diesen
      schwarten Himmel verlassen.
Auf der Kommode duften Äpfel, Grossmutter zündet
      goldene Kerzen an.'
                    (Georg Trakl: *Unterwegs*)

Above an urban landscape
lit by orange fires

a grey moth
is painted on the headboard
of the bed.
            It takes a lot

            to get into this bed; it costs
more than the industrialist-and-patron-of-the-arts
is prepared to pay; it takes love
(of a sort) and death (of a new kind)

but the one for whom it was first intended
has fallen asleep dead drunk
in a cradle of snow:

                  these are instances
and a family of stories springs from them –
a story of families
                    For

            *

to survive a night asleep
in the snow

betrays a determination to die
uniquely and only at the exact moment –

to fall, completed, like the fat mottled apples
grandmother used to store on the highest
shelf of the cavernous brown cupboard

which was so dark inside we expected
the smoke of an underworld
to escape into the kitchen. We imagined

that the apples *glowed* in that dark
when the cupboard door was shut.

*

An old water-colour hung from a nail
driven into the door. When
grandmother opened it to take out an apple

the picture would often crash to the floor –
its clouds and blue water writhing
to escape from the frame. This upset her.

She wanted to eat the apples in secret –
she did not want the children (whom
for the space of these songs 'we' are)
to know. We would sometimes surprise her

weeping inconsolably, leaning against
the big, black stove. We loved her
because her grief was always so mysterious.

In the water-colour an angel had almost
entirely faded, the strings of its harp
exposed like tendons.

*

On windy nights when the moon shook

she used to tell us about the old, abandoned
greenhouse lost among the black pine trees.

How had it arrived there? Dragged by the wind
its glass crackling among the stiff pine-
tops, disturbing the long, slow thoughts of the owl
and dropping when the wind dropped

turning and turning
down

shedding its orchids
into the enduring, blank leaves of a wilderness –
painted (perhaps) in a child's
book (this book?). And where had it come from?

– the City! We shivered
at the word. The lights of the City glowed
purple along the rim
of the furthest mountain range,
serrated like a leaf. Stars rose. White.

*

We argued for a long time –

who had been the first to discover
the dismantled piano

hanging from the beams of the garage
at our new house? What crashes and booms –

inexhaustible resonances! Even if
we all screamed at once its noise
could still drown us

like a wild night in a poem
('when the moon shook…').

We argued about the name of our new house.
Someone said 'lavender', others 'amber glass',
'purple', 'wishing cup' or 'perfume'.

We were very proud of the magnificent display
of bougainvillea that almost blocked the door.

*

It was lucky we never learnt
who our parents were.

Our lives were limitless, –
father a cloud, mother
a waterfall. Who could say

for certain we were not gods
or that one day we might not
inherit an Empire?

In the evenings we studied
the history of our dominions
in Asia.

                    *

When grandmother died
we imagined she had gone

into the black stove. From that time
religious observance declined in our family, –

besides, the sermons were boring, and since
we already knew everything about the stories
of Sodom and Gomorrah,

Vienna and Ur

we stayed home on Sundays to practise
our carpentry. O rosewood,
mahogany and oak! the pines also fell.

With each week the bed grew bigger and bigger.
Our work became famous, and as the news
spread so did a drowsiness

that occurred like the gradual perception
of a new colour, bleaching
its rivals in the spectrum. Sleep

followed, and the bed was full.

                    *

The nostalgia was so
irresistible

with its pictures of boats
scratched in charcoal

on pale skies and branches of white flowers
veined with pink

we did not notice it
was killing us. The point is:

if we had noticed would we
have taken any action
to prevent these developments, –

driving the bed back
into its trees? The
swoon

is all, like star-light
piercing

the worn linen
of a life.

                    *

But all of this happened in the angle of a mountain
or at the bottom of a lake, and there were other places
where red boulevards constantly sprang out or
retracted into the mouth of things, taking their trees

and lamp-posts with them. It was all movement –
blurred and fast enough to wreck the orchestra's
unison; a 'round' that landed the dancers miles
from the first pivot in a quite strange dance-hall

where the cloak-room attendants refused to understand
their questions. Cubes of steel and glass
were piled up along canals and quickly disguised
as churches or rotundas. But even these

melancholy attempts at continuity were soon
abandoned like the plans for a new 'Ringstrasse'
after the fall of the Empire. And this brought
elation or depression to people walking in the street,

and sometimes madness. Contradictory announcements
followed so quickly one on another that
everyone found themselves sleeping under news-print
imagining telephones in the night reaching

for glasses they had emptied. If it had been
possible sleep would have been abolished but somehow
people still needed – and needed more than ever
to dream of the lost, wealthy children,

the snow and the yellow apples, the waterfall
and the mysterious grief of the grandmother
leaning against the black lustre of the stove
where the winter salad was keeping warm.

Not that this altered anything or caused more
than a passing sense of loss as the next revolution
was hurriedly planned in the café. This was the life –
only, when the sky assumed a certain tone of grey

they knew that a moth had spread its wings, and when
the broken glass of a department store window
showered harmlessly against the shoulders of their
winter coats, they knew stars and the forest

had entered the town, the moon shaking in car tyres.

from **The Goodbyes**

Great Sonata I

The pianist commences the sonata about the angels and the rain.
It is so slow, so lingering we will soon be fast asleep

dreaming of pink rooms with musical animals and roses
while our teeth rot in sympathy, and outside
the autumn air grows dense as a preserving oil.

We must start now on the long route back
to 'the evidence of our senses' but it is hard, –
we may have to unlearn as much as we learn,

besides, we distrust all the approved maps and signposts…
So the threat arises of a sojourn as long as a life
in some commonplace purgatory
of cacophonous motels and braided intersections. Yet
these are not all that modern life has to offer us
and the town is not a monster to be run away from,
screaming into headlights and blank night: thus, escape
from one dilemma only lands us in the swamp
of another, and the smell is worse than ever…

We could invoke tradition, speed up the film of the flower
or imitate the procedures of music, in the hope
that these evasions might lead us, by way of doors
casually thrown open as if nothing were at risk

back to the dim point of departure. But how
can this appear as it was? It is only a confusion
of inclined planes, corridors and theatre boxes, –

a fake painting called 'Melancholy Of The Set-Square'.

American Bagatelles

An indestructible debris of plastics
burnt rubbers crushed metal

piled to the horizon's long drone

and above it in the isolation of a saint
a boy plays over and over
the chord beyond which his hand will not stretch.

*

The bombs have fallen
harmless as walnut shells
into the middle of the bathing party.

*

Strange, the customs here –

girls are buried with their boots on
and lockets round their necks
containing photographs of last year's boyfriends.

Note also the importance
of vehicles, water and musical instruments.

*

After the inspiring visit
of the semiologist
the citizen decided it was time to do something
about the crisis, – I mean the terrible boredom
everyone was feeling about then
even though the sky continued brilliant
and blue like the sky over Sounion.
It had gone too far;
it was getting into everything –
diluting the iced beers, corroding chrome bumpers,
swarming like a crowd bearing very dull placards
into any unattended space and refusing to budge

once established. Things were bad. No wonder
the kids had taken to satanism
and the worship of obscure fetishes...

        *

Billy came home with his head shaved and a mark
in the hollow of his cheek that would not scrub out
even with a stiff shaving brush. He was to die soon
in a country his terrified mother couldn't even imagine
as she stifled him with emotion, driving him out –
though this was the last thing she wanted to do –
on to the streets of the boring town where the drive-in
sold dildoes with onions, driving him into
the muscular arms of his charming friend Pete
who had admired, insincerely, the bleary water-colours
in which her son's gaunt face was constantly dissolving
into a landscape of unformed but very sweet desires.

        *

On scrubby hillsides
chalets and villas glimmer faintly,
ringing with cocktails...

The swimming pools are suspended
in mid-air
above the dry river bed.

The dead girl's uncovered face
stares up towards
the electric fences of her father's rose garden

and a chorus of young people stumbles away
through blue boulders,
retching, without an exit line

and still bored.

Them/There

to the memory of Erik Satie

What are the people like there? How do they live?...I'll admit I've never been there, but that won't stop me telling you all about it.

The people there weep often, alone in rooms with candles and old books. In their terrible Augusts they make black entries in their diaries. Their songs are doleful but the dances at funerals can be very lively, – danced to the rhythm of whips, gourds and snares – and the colour of mourning is ochre...They are fervently religious yet their government is atheist: to discourage worship the roofs have been removed from all their churches. But any government is provisional. Each summer, and sometimes during bad winters there are riots in the streets of their windswept and lacustrine capital. There are so many informers, however, that the police always know in advance the exact time and place. Thus everything is done properly: vendors may set up their stalls, street musicians choose their stands, and respectable families gather in perfect safety to watch the instructive spectacle...Tobacco and sheep are the basis of the economy. Out of patriotic duty everyone there chain smokes at incredible speed: they regard the medical reports with furious disdain, and their ceilings are stained a deep, yellowish-brown (like papyrus scrolls from the cemeteries of Fayyum). Their sheep are, without question, the shaggiest and most unkempt in the world, – each animal a mobile continent colonised by vast tribes of ticks...They are always washing things in water so soapy it is barely fluid, and yet nothing ever seems clean. And they think of themselves as Hellenes! Arbiters! ...In their typical symphonic music a huge, squelching adagio like a sea-slug is followed by epileptic dances, catastrophic marches, – the whole concluding in a welter of chromatic swoons. Their orchestras are very large. They play everything *fortissimo*. (And – horrors! – they re-orchestrate Mozart!) Their national anthem is an arrangement of the mastodon-trumpet theme from Scriabin's 'Poem of Ecstasy'. (When the massed bands of the Republic begin to play this it is difficult to persuade them to stop...) And yet, strange to relate, they possess singing voices of an exceptional and haunting beauty...Their buildings are either hen-coops or Piranesi dungeons, Nissen huts or Sammarran mausoleums...Their poets write constantly of their failed marriages, failing health, unhappy childhoods and – for variety – the apostrophes to stars of laundresses and cabmen...It rains often, yet the vegetation is sparse in many areas and the summers can be oppressively hot. Steam

43

rises in great clouds from their low roofs, and from the many balconies where drenched furs are hung to dry. Steam rises and moisture drips ceaselessly onto their unsurfaced streets in which a score of jeeps and hay-carts have their wheels stuck fast. Their flags hang always at half mast. As if ashamed their rivers vanish underground...In the south of the country there are extensive lakes of warm, grey mud...The train there moves in fantastic, slow loops, – a baroque embroidery expressing an infinite reluctance to arrive. They think, with good reason, that the world is forgetting them...They greet each dawn with a chorus of deafening expectorations.

Our Lives: A Symphony

1. Allegro ma non troppo

And these people have great wealth.
We should greet them in a fitting manner.
They have travelled here in coaches of a new design.
They are surrounded by indestructible glass.
They are like the most valuable exhibit in the museum, –
the gold mask, the only surviving fresco
from a tradition of three centuries. And they have seen
nothing to rival this. The evidence

of our poverty and great bitterness is
a new pleasure to them: the oaths thrown at them,
the stones are an entertainment, –
explosions of colour, savage music, dance-mania
you might expect to find in some obscure recess
of Empire, but not here at the centre
in ports from which the viceroys departed....

The parade crumbles,
and when an empty car goes up in flames
it is so surprising
it seems to be happening in slow motion:
it is still going on....

2. Adagio (lamentoso)

You have to pass under
so many derelict arches, –

viaducts, aqueducts

to reach the eastern rim
of the city
from which the transports leave

at increasingly infrequent intervals.
Not many wish to visit
and someone, one supposes, has to stay

since the buildings still stand
against the sky, solid and vacant

as cemetery statues. Our lives
have been folded away like a letter

bearing a message of terrible
urgency
and never posted.

3. Scherzo and trio

We love our city.
If we do not who will?

We have the biggest shopping-mall in Europe
and the biggest dispensing chemist

also the biggest hospital
the biggest mad-house, the biggest prison

the largest number of empty churches
and blocked canals (this –
of course – is the undiscovered Venice
the covert Petersburg
that Alexandria the sea snatched away...)

more beer is brewed here than in any other major city
and a blue mist envelops the tall buildings

the Japanese tourists
on the escalators ascend like saints, smiling
at magnificent blooms of smoke above the inner-suburbs.

4. **Molto moderato (quasi passacaglia)**

and the young couple emerge
from the hospital, its long façade
stretching for what seems a mile in either direction
of windows, windows…She
has one thin hand hooked over his arm (it
might be an empty glove) and she is carrying
a child wrapped in a plaid rug.

They descend the steps
and the town descends further before them, –
an infinite declension, darker and darker…
each ledge or street burdened with long ropes
of motionless people waiting
transport. The lights fail
briefly in a thousand windows
and resume, weakened. A woman

rounds a corner pushing a handcart before her,
and it is filled with dolls: small corpses,
each in a different, bright Victorian costume:
scarlet, mauve, yellow…

These are for sale, and a man shows
interest. He bends over them
and it must be that every vein in his face
has broken: engorged,

the nose pendulous, he fingers the synthetic
hair, and asks the price. On waking it is

the *price* dominates recollection,
its black and white stays fixed

like the first mountain you ever saw
or the first blood, the first death. Listening

into the night, you hear
a hammering, the nails are sinking in as windows
are blinded, and it still

goes on, even as sleep returns,
at no great distance, –

a wooden tapping (coffin lids)
a hammering....

Incidental Music

for Malcolm Scott

The musicians are writing letters of complaint.
They can't sleep, it keeps snowing in their hotel bedrooms.

Their instruments wait, tarnished in corridors,
for the polisher to come. Their shoes have left them

and winter follows them from Berlin
to Adelaide. During Schoenberg

the conductor mistakes a celesta
for a flexitone, and the sweat
from his tossed hair blinds the violas.

In Hong Kong one doesn't want to play Brahms
or talk to the ambassador's wife;

in New York one would prefer
to play a Symphony of Seven Stars
not pastorals for sheep...

There is general concern about
the anal fixation of the first trombone,
political agitation among the oboes
and drug abuse in the first violins –

rhythms drown in undifferentiated foam
and the new concerto from Sweden is
the equivalent in sound of wrapping paper and wet sand.

This isn't living. No, –
a museum should not be carried
on the backs of men,

and the musicians are writing letters of complaint
the musicians can't sleep

the musicians comb snow from their hair
the musicians refuse to play on the raft
the musicians are weeping the musicians are drunk –

with regret they have buried their instruments
in hope of better times.

A Beauty

It was not an intellectual face, –
white, with the mute look of a rose about to be doused
with a powerful insecticide,
and she never understood why, in her presence
perfectly sensible men would lose all control. What
was it she *did*? It cannot
have been anything she said…

Further incidents: she borrowed the old earl's Rolls
to take her to the station, and stole
his breakfast kipper to eat on the train;
the whole family had a wonderful time that summer
in the Tuscan palace lent by an infatuated count
except that all the floors were so highly polished
that, by the end of their stay, sprained wrists and broken ankles
were scattered through their ranks like floral tributes
at the end of a charity matinée;
she was horrified when her younger brother's hair
was cut short, declaring it 'an atrocity', –
and never forgot this…

Everything worried her, even the great rose-window of the cathedral, –
but there was always the consolation of 'the dear countryside',
rolling away like vellum or old velvet into a distance where,
unquestionably, something very nasty and probably foreign was
continually going on, – a kind of dust storm, an old argument
the wind wouldn't let drop, which she wasn't about to lend an ear to.

In 1917 Regie wrote to her: 'You remember Roughton?
Joined the Balloon Corps. Poor chap. Shot down
last week at 6,000 feet. He landed not far from me, –
shockingly foreshortened, but still recognisable by his cigarette case.'

The man she eventually married was a hopeless drunk.
She hardly seemed to notice. Despite this,
and his rumoured womanising, the marriage 'worked'.
During her second war she kept goats – 'such
useful animals' – and wrote to the ministry advising
the placing of giant magnets in the parks of the capital
to attract the German bombs there, –
'thus sparing many lives and many fine old buildings'.

Like her beauty, her myopia was legendary:
often she would sail past acquaintances of several years –
quite unawares, leaving a fine foam of grievances glittering in her wake.
In her extreme old age she still posed for photographs
wearing a large hat trimmed with brilliant blue ostrich feathers
(and this is a form of courage ought not to be disdained), –
her autobiography (ghost-written)
might have been called 'A Milliner's Chronicle', or
'The Philosophy of Hats', – recording, as it did,
the different phases of the horrible century she lived in
in terms of face-veils, lace-work, birds' wings, pins, and fake collapsing
    flowers:
a method not without advantages. As good as any, you might say...

Poor Boy: Portrait of a Painting

Difficult to say what all of this is all about.
Being young. Or simply arrogance, lack of patience –

a misunderstanding about what the word maturity
can mean when exchanged among 'real' adults...

I don't know what kind of plant that is, but it
is green and has a small red flower

and the glass it strives towards is latticed,
yellowish and cracked. Beyond it

roofs are bunched together like boats
in a popular harbour
and through it the inevitable light falls...

And the light is art! It is arranged *so*,
over the bed and the pale dead boy,
his astonishing red hair, the shirt rumpled like sculpture,

the breeches... The breeches are a problem:
no one can decide whether they are blue
or mauve. Versions differ. But the light

is faultless. It can hit anything
whatever the distance, –
for example, the squashed triangle of white lining
to the stiff, mulberry coloured dressing-gown,
the torn-up sheets of poems or pornography,
the oriental blade of pallor above
the boy's large, left eye-lid or even the small, brown
dope bottle lying on the scrubbed floor
almost at the bottom of the picture. Of course

much depends on the angle. Much remains
obscure, but this only enhances
these significant islands of brilliance,
exposed and absolutely
vulnerable to our interpretation:

there is nowhere he can hide the hand that rests
just above his stomach as if he still felt horribly ill.

The Stranger in the Corridor

'O sole, true Something – This! ...'
    S.T. Coleridge

With vague attributes, they all wander in here
at one time or another. Often
I wish they would stay longer, if not to speak,
then perhaps to take on some more certain form, –

a swirl of colour (orange or green) in an otherwise
transparent marble that has just emerged,
of its own volition, from years of exile under the sofa.
And why has it come to us at this moment?

The unimpressive apparition might mean something, –
for an unexpected pause in the recitation of a letter
can have more power to disturb than a whole succession
of subsiding Valhallas, and we can barely read the words

announcing the discovery of the lost girl,
the mystery of the mésalliance. Is it the dim light?
Or tears of the sort that are compared to pearls? ...

We care about this more than a little
but will never know: this evening's visitor comes as an odour
of freshly baked bread that follows me
down the narrow corridor from the little bedroom lined with books,
and there is nowhere it can come from! It seems
friendly enough, 'concerned' even. A response from the air.

Or something that has stepped outside of me for a moment
to 'take the air' like a fluttering heroine after the execution
of some especially fevered nocturne, in search of refreshment
to stretch its limbs a little, and to remind me that I have been

Neglecting it. And I *have* been neglecting it. This is obvious,
for it most resembles a guest at a crowded party whom you have
        introduced to no one:
a charming guest but with a look of reproach.

I have forgotten so many things and this is one
and wants to take its place among the salvaged, –
among flowers from the fifties or the colours of a paintbox,
under the brim of a hat, beside a gold river at the heart of an old
      province
that is growing with each intake of breath
as the fresh odour spreads, claiming the most impervious objects,
reviving the colours that had begun
to fade to white scarves of the death of this place
that is now big as a democracy, vivid as a nettle's sting, –
and we cry out, hurt! The task ahead
is momentous but pleasurable: you have to invent, or –
which may be the same thing – remember
the language of this place, its peculiar history, cuisine and carnivals;
what people did in its eighteenth century; whether it is
appropriate to talk of 'serfdom' after the close of its nineteenth century,
the ambiguous relationship of this to the rise of a bourgeoisie...
And so on. You might also prepare new
and superbly accurate editions of dissonant masterpieces
by its early church composers, or discover
in a foxhole, the last act, lost for decades, of its most famous opera.
When you have done all this, conducted a census
and completed the catalogue of native birds, you will be able
to find the place where, in the midst of this much folded and
pleated landscape   the loaf rises like a monument:

now free from hunger and confinement,
we inhabit its shadow.

Antique Emotions

Perambulant flowers, snow-
sculptures, soap dishes:
the hostess blames them for her sleeplessness;
the dinner guests cover their ears.
They go on singing, poor birds,
in the middle of the lake and
are not understood. Each auditor

resembles the aborigine first
confronted by
a serenade from Salzburg, –
the movements passing swiftly far
above, like blurred constellations, –
beautiful in their blue way but
referring to different myths,
ones he couldn't sing:

'You do not understand
the profound love we feel for one another
and for you. And this
is the principle of our society, its
glittering podium: our colour signifies
our selflessness, our wings close over
the young we are denied and at nightfall
we are possessed in terror by the foreknowledge
of our deaths. But this too will be given
if it is demanded by you –

you grounded at some distance, on
terraces, in houses, in the light.'

And the cry goes up from the table:
'Enough! Pass the red beans, the rough wine.'

The Threshold Moment

with acknowledgements to the Chic Organisation

The continual, gnawing dissatisfaction of people patrolling a basement
looking into each others faces and finding nothing
was glossed by the music. 'Rebels!…Rebels!…' The refrain
nearly finished us. But now, in time for you to breathe, the entertainment
    collapses, –
a coloured tent, the poles protruding all ways, the cloth drenched. And
    here,
sprouting carnivorous flowers of mould, are volumes one to the infinite

of the world's saddest and most boring stories, sagas of perpetual
	disappointment, –
the right one always eluding, a kind of Cinderella syndrome
with an enormous surplus of princes and ugly sisters...

Speak to the owl, if you can find one. The jig is up. Our ideas have left
	us, –
they were at the bottom of the glass. And something opens to a great
	depth,
like the blue of the sky when birds are lost in the severe alps of commerce.
A kind of regressive feeling sets in, like an ache. Time to go home.
Only...a certain, over-reaching ambition remains, –

to go further, refusing to accept this as the end point, signalled by old,
	deafening clocks,
leaving the chaste houses of parents and professors far behind,
as a thin mirage drawn on the air by sombre children good at sums;

to be lost from sight, shameless monomaniacs, recognising only what
	we touch –
what touches us – the small tremor in which the world consents to be
	extinguished
as a pot of flowers (geraniums perhaps) is extinguished
when it falls from the sill of a high tenement window: something
remains, but nothing you'd recognise. But you exaggerate (and *why
	not?*)
you are thinking of Italy or some other place of light, and floral tributes
where the legend is: 'These people really know how to live.'

You may take pleasure in feeling lost, but, of course, you remember
how quickly we can traverse the long way back, knowing
all the brambles and wires by rote, – knowing too well
those ravines like lying smiles of welcome that would swallow us, until
we arrive at the place where the new day romantically extends
its pale and still cold hand with an old-fashioned courtesy like lace...

And it is a promontory where trees have rooted in the stacks
of an abandoned library now barely distinguishable from the space
	around it,
and a staircase leads down from the dust of the central door
towards the distant city, which naturally only *seems* distant:
it is almost in your hand, – a kind of cubist garden wherein

a crowd of people move at blurring speed, under foliage of smoke,
among pillars built with mirrors, reflecting vast sunsets.

Or it is only the memory rising from some such name
as Ctesiphon, or the chessboard of Ch'ang-an, Tu Fu lamented...
But no, it is real, you insist, and the musty names I drag up depress you.
Look, the ocean is receding from the streets and squares
and those who have slept awake! It is another legend, another fable,
one that ends happily. And each individual –
their clothes, their hair or the small movements of their hands,
impresses us as the element of a pattern we wouldn't, just now, alter a
     stitch,
although we know sadness is in it like an ink-stain. The conquest

has been accomplished, and no one was subjugated. I am, you are
eager for the oncoming night, – its lights, its advertisements, the sound
     of its cars...
The sky looks like storm clouds: each of us conducts lightning.

Music Understood by Children and Animals

If the wasp is stuck in the wet disk of blue
in the open paint-box we won't be able to paint
our breathtaking adventures on the horizon, –

the place the bird-calls come from: their truth would be in doubt, –
also it seems a discourtesy not to know the names
of these singers whose cries are like coloured flares, burning
on a wide circumference by which we judge direction
and scope. But now, the blistered sills are hot
and we're listening and leaning into a distance that's
immense, capable of any transformation –

How far? How deep? Who will come with us?
Everything is in there, even the mountain
where the elephants go to die. Sad, the elephant songs
in the morning. We'll come back with their bones
and with them build huts in the water-meadows:
we'll live on marigolds, on marigolds. Ivory will keep us...

Now the ballet's about to begin. The signs are hung
at a friendly distance and the dew dries on them.
The clear air's full of the feeling of curtains rising
and everyone's ears are tuning up. The woods
are wrapped in a new colour, unmentioned in the shade-card
and the statues are hidden beyond nettle-patches. Their
fallen hands have been carried off finger by finger
by field mice and buried: they always looked ill...

When the bell strikes we pull in our heads
and the world composes itself like a deep pool
around the angel from Italy, the chrome flowers in the vase, –

we're kneeling in a room but we're somewhere else
there's a ceremony but the pauses
and orations are measured behind our shut lids

we're found we're lost we're sinking we're rising
like bubbles from fish-mouths like feathers on a breeze
in so many depths of blue turning to violet –

and it begins

like a song like a stomach ache like a sleep
like a haze of heat. How far? How deep?

If the river falls over a cliff that is high enough
it will never reach the ground: it will end
in rainbows a hundred feet up.

Early Views of Manchester and Paris: Third View

A Venetian palazzo, a Roman temple, a French chateau, a dome from
a mosque in North Africa...Cast-iron capitals in the form of lotus
flowers, gable-ends, dormer windows (after Mansard), chimneys like
vases, – the solid memory of smoke...Continent of geometric forms
gleaming darkly after the rain inhabited by democratic communities of
birds...ô ville que l'on dit industrielle...here are the green canals of
childhood...

You are approaching a news-stand, and you look up. And there, flooded in a sunlight denied to the street's depths, balconies curve outwards, pilasters taper or swell towards leaves encased in scrolls... a Titan blows a conch and windows break upwards through the architrave that should limit them... The dictionary of architecture lies open, in three dimensions.

(In the city our idea of 'the country' is conditioned by camera angles and peasant costumes in dull productions of Chekhov: even allowing for our ignorance, it cannot be *so* interesting...)

Also there are places where shadowy columns rise towards inscriptions in dead languages, and they are like film-sets waiting for the ultimate crowd scene, – the entry into Rome or Thebes, the banquet at Persepolis – which now can never be filmed. Alas! the producers have gone into tax-exile... So the space remains unoccupied but for the slow accumulation, in colourless layers, of puzzled speculation concerning forbears who required such a gulf between a dim, blue ceiling and the conduct of their business.

Crowds. Collisions. Dusty parks. Red tulips.
Abstract street-battles. Muted, sexual outcry.

Sometimes it is as if the whole of life were lived in the sub-basement of a department store, among packing-cases and forgotten typewriters. The buildings stand imbued with sadness. The last firework has exploded in the night-sky of summer and the children know that tomorrow the work begins, the confinement...

Patrons, captains and pay-masters! The city would like you to appreciate its recent attempts at efficiency and self-criticism, – its severe new face of yellow brick. Like a convert to an unforgiving faith it divests itself: the old statues and ropes of stone flowers are pounded into a dust that clogs the ventilation systems of its half-empty hotels...

place où ma vanité devait se pavaner... I can neither forgive nor forget any of this.

The Goodbyes

1   Again, the weather's wrecked the picnic.
All those drenched frocks,
tomato slices in flooded bowls –

so English! the clouds, the downpour
as evasive terms
for a continuing epic of bad faith
and commonplace ill-feeling...

2   Yes, something *has* changed
irreversibly. It speaks out of silence
like a radio announcer
off-cue. Time to remove the varnish? Yes...

3   All departures cancelled:
the pillars in the painting are grey
and the sails of fishing boats
drawn in with no hope of unfurling, –
blue cranes of the container-depot
motionless. Only the immense
sandstone cathedral looks as if it might move –
gliding off, a gothic liner, leaving
the city burning behind it...

4   Dun cows like stalled cars
are dumped in all the streams:
someone has *smoked* the landscape.

5   The glass graph-paper of office buildings catches
no sun this evening, and this expresses
everything we feel about the situation and do not understand, –

How could you love a person like him or like her?
They are ignorant, – they think *all* Italians are Catholic.
Their blond hair gets into everything, even sleep...

6   With things as they are it's difficult not
to feel like a newly arrived exile
even though you've lived here for years.
Principal cities are renamed and history

slides into a dull dream of foreknowledge
in which past mistakes are cancelled.
Who are these heroes appearing in the false guise
of youth? these avatars of
expediency? No one is convinced. Even
the sky is discoloured
like the pages of a novel left open at a window, –
the plot so mechanical every word or sigh
fell with a thud to rot slowly where it fell,

staining the carpet at the place
where the corpse is marked in chalk.

7 And the clouds! The clouds!
    O, a thousand sobbing goodbyes!

    Overweight and weeping bitterly
    they are dragged off to interrogation:

    they confess everything,
    including your address...

8 A fog is expected, –
    the first 'real pea-souper' in years.
    'You can't rely on the weather...'
    Everyone agrees on this
    while the window darkens
    like someone's mother's brow in splendid
    anger: 'Child! O
    ingrate! My lichen! Little cuckoo, go
    into the world: it is
    a narrow corridor and we do not know its end, –

    unless it be this blurred picture
    of a river or a tree, branching in Africa...'

9 Voices rise in confusion, –
    counterpoint of amateurs. Talk
    turns to the furniture of permanence.
    Contracts are signed, houses change hands
    (hands change houses) but yours
    is not (is never) the face seen at the window

advertising with a cold smile
its new contentment. That smile! You'd think
death were abolished, and people
not starving with infinite slowness –
là-bas, là-bas: their hands make a thorn-bush
on which your morning paper is impaled.

10   Friend, you'd better board up that window,
never know what might go down to-night –

an ice factory is planned for your garden
a steel mill for your living room
a six-lane highway for the hall
and even now, directly beneath your feet
huge coal-seams are being explored...

The walls are shaking. The light
is drunk. Goodbye.

11   This is only goodbye –

a handkerchief like a white wing
a tear in a bottle, a moist hand
encountered in a hotel foyer,

the goodbye of silence,
late music and exhausted nerves

goodbye stretched to the furthest point
of perspective, where
the small spaces of our lives
submit to immensity –

the grass that continues as an unbroken blue undulation
over mountain ranges and stepped cities of moss

the goodbye of calls
crossed and misdirected
like the preparatory sketch
for the beast in a fable, –

bearded with sharp ears
the face a kind of mesh that shines towards us
as the goodbye
of everything we are uncertain of

the goodbye that leaves you ruined
(split cast for a bronze figure of defeat)

the goodbye of goodbyes
it wants no more –

the goodbye of words
that rub themselves out

the goodbye like a blank staircase leading
back into whatever you were.

Ferns and the Night

'Und wir hörten sie noch von ferne
Trotzig singen im Wald.'

This is the sort of place you might arrive at after a long journey
involving the deaths of several famous monsters,
only to be disappointed almost to the point of grief.

Heavy clouds hang in a clump above a wide, perfectly level plain
which is the image of a blank mind. Night is falling.
There is a wooden house, a lighted porch: it is a scene of 'marvellous
    simplicity'. –
too marvellous perhaps: the very grain of the wood offers itself
for our admiration, and the light has such 'warmth'
it is hard to restrain tears. The clouds are now distinctly purple,
agitated, – a kind of frantically stirred borsch, suitable backdrop
for some new opera's Prelude of Foreboding, but not for this ambiguous
    scene
of severity tempered by domestic tenderness, in which we find
the 'young mother' looking for her child…He has run off

into deep woods nearby, leaving his blue train crashed on the lawn.
She calls his name, but after the third call it becomes difficult or exotic
    music,
a series in retrograde inversion, an entry in the catalogue of unknown
    birds:
she is already elsewhere, her torch illuminating the pure,
chlorophyll-green ferns of a forest, and the torch itself, a flame...

She finds that her bare feet are wet and that she is looking into a puddle,
Seeing the clouds reflected and her face (the moon also). She calls again
but has forgotten where she is, or whose name she is calling. Her own
    perhaps?
The wooden house, the lighted porch seem unreachable, –
artfully lit, a glassed-in exhibit in some future museum of the human.
Ferns and the night conceal the child whose laughter distantly reaches
    her.

Great Sonata 2

Call it a river, –

call it a summer or an open house:
a mild rain is falling through sunlight onto benches
shrubs and a fountain, – characters
in this story that is not a story. Strangers
are welcome here, and you have finally walked out
of that mean and dusty apartment you once called
a self. The air tastes good, doesn't it?
And you won't need your books or records with you
since, now, you can recall them all at will –
the words, the notes will no longer seem like props
but will be free structures in which you can loiter, or not
as the mood takes you. Similarly,
you will like the people here but if you choose
to ignore them no offence will be taken. A lake
is nearby, unseen, but altering the light falling across your knees
and, like an unjust tax, the accent of regret is abolished.

But see...the fountain doesn't work any more
and the strict plan, though admirable, can't
be imitated: it is just one of many things
that elude us or are 'gone for ever', like rosewater down a sink...

Yesterday's a spectre in classical dust sheets.
Today's a lad dressed with ragged insouciance.
And a new quality of attention is needed: silences
have to be orchestrated, portraits drawn with invisible ink
if we are to know what is really taking place
beyond this pale surface that is so satisfying in itself...
Some minor romantic heroine may be dying
in a bare, panelled room no one ever visits, or
perhaps a child has lost his way in the blue woodlands of an illustrated
    book
and now the brambles come alive to bind his ankles, –
or it may be that some buried hope, that once seemed foolish,
is about to issue forth to demand immediate
construction of the forms it can live in: now it is *the only rational
    solution*...
a loggia by Brunelleschi, a portico by Inigo Jones
in which the evening light of a summer, not far from the Aegean
has been permanently installed.

Meanwhile the sun has risen again,
like a chord in C, through bars of cloud;
and everyone is still looking into that garden
or walking in some other garden or park
exchanging words about
the flower bed in the shape of a clock-face, –

and it really tells the time –
our time, in generous periods like Schubert.

from The Branching Stairs

D'abord il faut désobéir: c'est le premier devoir quand l'ordre est menaçant et n'explique pas.

Maurice Maeterlinck, from his libretto for Dukas' opera *Ariane et Barbe-Bleue*

The Saying Goes

The legend of that relationship had been going on
for so long, – longer than any river –
it might have been written in Langue d'Oc

and in a small, crapulous town full of absurd hoardings
dominated by a leaning water-tower
they found themselves, at last, without either food
or money, half blinded by the flying dust,
bitumen and grit. But even this amused them,
and abashed townsfolk who had held back, awaiting
the outcome of the arrival, soon emerged,
crab-like, from weathered houses to fill big cans
from the wall-fountain their laughter had become.

'Without visible means of support'
they were immortal, the arms of a constellation at least.
'Of no fixed abode'
they were the longed-for home,
novel in design yet commodious, suspended above
the cataract of great changes. Their throats
desert-dry, their lips parched and cracking,
they were still a musical
with lavish scenes of rain and kissing.

At the end of the street a sigh or sign said 'The End',
but it lied unless the world is a passage, and you know
it is more like this story although less blithe;
it is like a way of thinking, interrupted on occasion
by lacunae of sleep and dreaming when a gauze
falls in front of the severe platform, shifting the figures,
merging the arcs that represented discrete events in time,
but always resuming until the mind dies. And, then, flowers are given

and towers of solitude are raised
at regular intervals across the declining land

and it begins again in another mind
like a benign empire with laws, cities, provinces.

The Philosophies of Popular Songs

   for Brinley Mitchell

1

That day things turned out well: not as foreseen –
since there was no place to fit you in the map
I had drawn on the carton. There may have been
omens, but no one had remembered to consult
the clouds, the entrails, the pattern of leaves around
the fondly-remembered-sundial or the dreams
of frightened wives. The mask of reason remained
where it was, smiling on the keystone of the arch.

At most there was the chance of falling down
later, in the evening, among the damp cardboard
piled up in alleyways, again mistaking
streetlamps for planets, imagining the distinguished stranger
with the plain jewellery was showing interest again:
not much of a festival – no balloons, O sad kermesse!

You should have worn flowers. White ones.
Some pink. Or a chain. A leather helmet.
A badge announcing your unusual splendour –

before the performance began and everyone was expunged from view
while sighing deeply as if they had lost something
beyond the price and were about to find it again – *there*
on the stage, the moment the lights came up
revealing the pale receding landscape I had designed
to be viewed through the shattered windows
of a French cathedral...

        and yes that dull smudge
like used soap is someone's face laughing or crying.

2

The performance was a full one.
It was thrilling.
But would we get through?

Part 1. Exercises In Style
Part 2. Songs On The Death Of Children
Part 3. Anthropological Sambas/ The Sacrifice
Part 4. Quatre Chansons Paysannes

– and you the unannounced fifth, the chord
introducing the colours of the painted forest.

Now hold it! as if this were a photograph
and cameras still primitive.
Don't tremble. It won't die. Not *ever*.

3

Trees shadowed the columns of the white porches
Around the square down a street or two

The telephone rang in its kiosk
Unanswered on the corner

There were flowers at the station entrance
Rising in tiers towards a brown arch

The foyer was hushed though crowded
We were damp with a light sweat pretending to be rich

Stark furniture and very walls were vocal
We knew the words to that song

Believing them everyone since in that altered air
The blandest lie would stifle and expire

And the night deepened like a sound
In the velvet registers of an orchestra

4

But the embrace. The obscure journey.
The bed. The nest of curls. The stem.
The tall buildings with their mirrors and kitchens.

Darkness under the trees and bridges.
The empty shirts emblazoned by the early sun
with chevrons. I won't describe these. You know them

or you remain in exile. The true question
is moving out into this day (the next one),
spreading like a level ocean through the streets,

its colours uncertain. You are unsteady.
You'd like to take off your shoes. You'd like to lie
under the sprinkler before insurance offices

reflecting the heavens. You'd like to sleep, at last,
in ignorance, since no maps cover the delta
whose distributaries now depart from you.

But the alarm keeps howling in the locked car,
and follows you. And you begin to forget.

Snow: A Romance

No. That is the sun. *This* is a blood-orange.
I eat the orange, the sun goes down.
Or, I eat the sun, the orange goes down?...

He sees the resemblance everywhere. It is his trade, his survival technique –

(The pines are German philosophers, impoverished misanthropes.)

most particularly he understands the close affinity between complete stillness, and movement so rapid it deceives the eye. And he can listen. The blades of a helicopter turn in a ravine. What does that tell him?

He finds the girl in the snow. Only he has seen her. She is so white, only a shred of bright hair might provide a focus for rifle-sights. In a split second, moving more quickly than a lizard, he has snatched her away. She is icy cold. If she is not to die he must carry her quickly down to the lake.

At first she is tiny and silent. He feels that he could fold her up and slip her into the inside pocket of his coat, next to the gun and the passport. But as the air grows warmer, as they rapidly approach the lake, and fear dies away (for her bemused pursuers are still searching with long sticks for the scrap of gold they lost in the drifts) she seems to grow larger and heavier. Now she is like a basket of rye-loaves, now like a bundle of furs, now like kindling or laundry, now like a harvest gathered in quickly to avoid the first frosts. And she begins to sigh. She begins to hum a little. It is as if power had been restored to a machine left abandoned for years, and to everyone's surprise it still works, still gives light and warmth, and a song by Brahms. Now she can walk, unassisted, and they descend together towards the ever-more-deeply-blue-lake as evening comes down like a single enormous iridescent wing.

She is now much taller than the man who, next to her, resembles some small animal – a lizard for example. Indeed a cloud obscures her brow. Indeed a star gets tangled in her hair. A star falls when her shoulder grazes it. A shooting star! So

pure and lost! all the people gathered round band-stands by the lake look up in wonder and call out across the motionless water towards the peaks behind which it vanishes.

*

The hotel reminds him somehow of a paddle steamer. A wooden balcony runs the length of the first floor punctuated by trellises and tubs of small anxious-looking flowers (for a severe frost or late fall of snow is still possible at this time of year) and terminated at either end by domed octagonal turrets. There are also some national flags and close to the principal, low-arched entrance an incongruous neon sign announcing Bureau de Change.

He hires the largest suite, but a design of snow-drops on the wallpaper strikes him as a bad omen. He frowns. It is late (the soft sound of a tuba is heard from the lakeshore), and she falls asleep immediately. Once again she becomes very small, curled like the ear of a mouse in the enormous, heaped bed. Sadness overcomes him and he retreats to an armchair with whisky and a book. By dawn she is hardly more than a wisp of smoke. Now anxiety grips him: by now assassins must have found their trail. He checks the balcony and scans the park below. Clipped bushes, pollarded trees, curving paths (the whole in the shape of a star or sharp-petalled rose) and nowhere is there any sign of assassins. Naturally, he concludes that they must be concealed everywhere like dragons in a child's picture puzzle. The scene becomes hard with menace as if enamelled. The situation requires immediate action.

(The local police, he knows, will be of little use: such is their contempt for the criminal classes they will not give them the satisfaction of betraying the slightest interest in their activities. This is an old resort of great refinement, heroic gentility: dowagers, novelists, aesthetes flock here to die of the right diseases. The chief industry is the production of memoirs.)

He gathers her up in the folds of a dressing-gown, and dodging swiftly through the foyer, joins a party of tourists moving uneasily with them towards the pleasure park on the shore. He tips her gently into a chair of the ferris wheel. There they will not notice her; they will not see her in the blur of the wheel.

Having fashioned a deadly blow-pipe from a light-fitting he sets out to explore the town. And they are everywhere! In the new shopping-mall, in the cathedral (lurking behind the massive piers of its Burgundian romanesque), in the parks, in tree-lined streets and squares, in taxis, in telephone kiosks and sewers, under the Jugendstil arch of the railway stations... and silently, with incredible speed he kills them all! With faint cries they drop from the branches of trees...

It has been a good day's work. But when he returns to her he finds that the constant turning of the wheel has strangely lightened her: she floats home like a balloon attached to the cuff of his shirt. All night she floats just below the level of the ceiling. Only at dawn does she drift down to settle on his naked chest. Is she beginning to love him? It is impossible to know: her face is too perfect to be legible, and so far she has not said a word.

*

Early morning. A low rumble as of stage-machinery. He knows assassins have returned numberless as ever. He looks out. The light is null. Certain shadows in the park are uninterpretable, and surely it is too early for a boy to be circling aimlessly on his bike? Do his eyes deceive him? Snow seems to be falling although it is now high summer. Only the lake speaks clearly: the sun rising above a savage serration of peaks, strikes its centre; light dances fantastically over the stucco flowers of the ceiling – the lilies, the Ottoman tulips. Their petals seem to move, to breathe. So the solution strikes him: today she will be an untidy bouquet such as fond boys take to their mothers, nothing more. They will escape by boat towards the southern mountain range that so resembles a line of women dreaming – it is called 'The Women'.

It seems so simple. They are already in their boat. He rows furiously. The muscles of his arms dance, and the sun shines on them. But she begins to grow heavier and their boat hangs low in the water. They are at the centre of the lake heading south and the water reaches his lips. Surely he will drown, and for what? They will be two corpses interlocked on a dank mandorla of weeds. His hair is already floating on the surface of the water (where it resembles a strange and beautiful plant), and this is perhaps the low point of his life, when suddenly he feels himself borne up (and once again she is growing) carried high into the air! Water cascades from their bodies. They are like the statues of a fountain. She cradles him and continues, with immense strides, their journey to the south. At last he relaxes completely. Perhaps this is what he has been looking for – the love of a kind giantess who has no need of him at all. The world is now as open and welcoming as the field of her hair. The nets in which he wound himself unwind: they fall like ruined lace. Does she love him? Soon she will speak, in her own time. Her first words will be: 'Man, why did you come looking for me? I was not in any danger.'

Life Under the Table

The monster came up out of the rain –
oh help! – like something vomited
from the dank depths of the gooseberry swamp,
all hirsute and dripping. In terror,

the watchers ran under the table and began
to enjoy themselves with a good deal
of exaggerated cowering: would it help, they wondered
if they covered themselves with a net of vines

or other leaves, presuming any could be found?
Of course, it was only the neighbours' imbecilic hound
in a specially rambunctious mood, and
the accurate trajectory of an old boot soon put it to flight

(just as the same boot, kept by for such
purposes, had once saved the life of a thrush
caught in the mouth of a startled cat) but they
refused to believe it: they would not come out –

and even the appeals of respected public men
(debouching in haste from helicopters)
were met with remarks of such a hurtful
and cynical nature, thrown

altogether like a basketful of arrow-heads
that they retreated in tears. They
(the watchers) liked where they were: limits
were clearly set; bores could be excluded,

and also persons with unpleasant personal habits.
Their belief in the monster hardened –
assuming the character of a dogma.
They detailed its vile attributes, even imagining

they saw pools of blood and the tears of mothers:
thus something like a religion was born,
with a novel conception of heaven, and no hell
but what was 'real' beyond the stout,

spiral legs at the four corners of the kingdom,
and from this sprang a rich artistic tradition.
Before the world finally forgot them
it was observed that they had begun to paint

on the underside of the table
a bright blue sky, scattered with gold stars
and the episodes of an epic
were creeping remorselessly across the carpet.

Bespalko's Devotions

1

The rivers do not announce themselves,
passing almost silently,
the land hardly dips towards them.

A crumbling wooden jetty marks a vanished crossing
a barge in the shallows has sunk as far as it will go.

Call it lack of ambition, vainglory or skill
the centuries of our indigence
left no enduring monuments. Under

a clear October sky
a line of aspens...

a line of palings weathered into grey
and vanishing under sand,
a spring of sweetwater wasting itself

speak to the observant of a former village –
oh, in the whisper of a dialect
banned from the schools. And the villagers?
Their labour was required elsewhere.

As to our ancestors, the images of their gods
are crude and featureless like the wooden dolls
a beaten child will talk to in its misery,

yet their princes' names are as splendid
as the names of the kings of Parthia or Kushan,

they survive in tales of The Aspen Witch,
The Jewelled Pike In The White Ponds,
The Tree That Weeps On The Moon.

2

The summer trees are dark where the yellow oriole sings.
Exiles are writing their sonnets to autumn.

Walking back from the post office,
clutching parcels of censored mail
they glance uneasily at the sky.

In the evenings they drink and talk:
they depict with longing
the terraces of the secretariats,
the ministries' many revolving doors,

the flowers and cedars of Fountain Park,
the intellectual cafés, the cabarets,
and swallows under the eaves of the Summer Palace.

Also they denounce the government,
the corruption of the capital.

They drink and they talk and they count –
hours, days, miles and seasons. They fear
the rigours of our winters, the wide streets frozen
and open to the winds, the walls leaking cold.

They count and they talk: no one listens,
children are warned against them
for sedition is dangerous, and, innocent
as they seem, they are not trusted.
They who could choose, chose badly.

In the night they press their ears
to ancient radios only to hear
themselves or their friends condemned.

They fear the time when they cease to recognise
the names in the anathemas.

3

The river mist deepens. The fields are cold.
It is not your shadow alone that follows you
darkening the reeds at the edge of the pond.

But no, again I tell you, the witch
will not rise above the poles of the wells

and you come bearing an apple
cold to the touch, red as a peony.

O the house in the apple tree,
the tree in the cloud,
the cloud that carries the star away,
the star in the basin, the moon in the lake!

The white water washes my soul clean
the white water drowns me.

Herons rise like ghosts
above the flooded fields.

Having Windows

for Judith Ennew

High on these cool hill-tops,
tonight in this suburb of a thousand flowers
no sentimental ordinances pertain, –
gardeners must attend to our boredom,
exchanging the red roses for the yellow

and the yellow for the white,
plagued with moths, quietly in a kerosene light.

Every prospect must accord with our views
which are orderly and proper, only
each day the garden must alter a little (no,
not those massed pinks and tearful blues)
hence these curses and soft songs rising at midnight
to terraces from which we like to admire sunsets
that match the colours of our cocktails.
In discussion with our architects we dream of pools,
guest pavilions and electric gates.

But somehow every project fails
breeze-blocks and scaffolding litter the streets,
cement sets in useless piles, and what was new
last year is ruinous today,
drifted with dust like worn-out snow,
and sometimes a mist blows
in from the sea to hang above us
like the recollection of a crime; it clothes us as we sleep, –
sorrowful animal that loves us,
it stays, it stays, is never released in rain
but lifts in time, and then

you would not believe the vistas
that fan out, like a hand of cards, from our
vast windows, windows filling entire walls:
to the east a narrow desert, endless blue Sierras,
below us to the west, the city we abandoned, –
wrecked baroque stage-set, smudged in its pall
of dust and smog (beyond it the land falls
towards an ocean that divides the world)
and far to the south rising in dim mounds, treeless
like spoil heaps, the regions of poverty, –
habitations of the windowless...

When we glance in that direction
we briefly bless the good fortune
that gave us such splendid windows, –

for there, things have sunk so far
few can afford the glass or the iron bars
against robbery, and window spaces
are closed roughly with discarded bricks.
Except in thin shafts striking the can
kept for the daily water trucks,
a forehead glazed with sweat or a cooking pan,
light rarely penetrates those thousand distant rooms,
and on days of sea-mist the women
and young children might be entombed
(one imagines it a scene for Caravaggio
or Zola) and they grow pale, they grow
as pale as the rich once affected to be
who now lie prone whole weekends by the sea,
as a swift, cold current passes their feet.

And it has become fashionable
to regard this new pallor of the poor –
who only recently laboured to plant crops and dig
incalculable miles of irrigation ditches, –
as 'beautiful'. But I cannot approve of the fad, for
I declare it to be a perversion of aesthetics
which even boredom cannot adequately excuse, –
for who would go so far
as to observe closely, still less to touch
this disenfranchised loveliness? No,

we must thank God for our gardens
and our windows, marvellous windows
which give us the liberty to gaze down
in all directions, like sea-birds or weather-vanes
at evening, when an unforgiving sun
ignites the panes.

The Ruins, with Phrases from the Official Guide

for Christopher Middleton

A city: prosperous and clean,
closely ringed by low, wooded hills, –
neither too small nor too large
it possesses 'all the civilised amenities'.

Its inhabitants are noted
for their love of music and confectionery.
They are proud of their city. They spend
much time attending to their window-boxes,
or signing petitions demanding
stricter control of effluents in the famous river
that winds convulsively through their city
like the signature of a prize-winning author...

And this river, to add to its picturesqueness,
is adorned with a group of islands known as
'The Necklace'. On two of these islands
are public gardens and cafés screened by willows,
on a third is an old fortress 'of grim aspect',
on a fourth (the largest) are a church
and numerous houses of an extinct nobility;
the fifth is hardly more than a rock, crowned
with the statue of a florid woman weeping
as if for a dead son or lost lap-dog.

The city's historic buildings
'date mostly from the seventeenth and eighteenth centuries', –
they are uniformly elegant, never too
oppressively grand, and the many small houses,
that wear their window-boxes
like strips of embroidery on the costumes
of peasant women posing for tourists, are built
of wood and rose-coloured brick. It is all

charming. But a peculiarity
strikes the visitor, – a mystery. It is
as if a beautiful piece of cloth, perhaps
a banner, a stole or a cope,

were spotted with an inexplicable decay
which no one had thought to repair. Or
perhaps a superstitious fear prevented them...
for at various points in the heart of the city,
beside the smart, new buildings and the elegant old ones
stand ugly ruins, without dignity,
sprouting weeds as nostrils sprout hairs
and sealed off with coils of barbed wire, –

one flight of a staircase clings half way up
a precipice of blackened brick, hideous wallpaper
hangs in strips like partially flayed skin,
dust-caked windows are broken, girders
protrude like stumps. These are left as a reminder, –
but of what? – of some ineradicable
corruption, some great violence in the past,
like sites of mass burials?... The visitor
begins to regard the very paving stones he walks on
with some suspicion (where are the bones,
the mats of hair, the lime pits?...) and at
the mere mention of the subject the inhabitants lose
all their renowned geniality and frankness.
Imagine, if you will, someone who does not believe in ghosts,
who sees one, and still will not admit the truth of it.

Of course one must presume such charming people
innocent, and perhaps one should ascribe the ruins
(which are so calculated in their disorder
they might be fakes) to the ancient wisdom
of the city fathers who wish to remind us only
that all cities are mortal, that even this most
prosperous, most impeccably bourgeois of cities
will go the way of Ephesus and Antioch,
of Tanis and Sakala. But a doubt remains:

a city is not an axiom.

A Letter from the Dwarf

Forgive me if I write hurriedly. I am anxious to set down the things I have to say to you before I forget them. A minute ago they seemed important but now – well, I don't know…However I will continue to write even if I can no longer remember why I should find my lost pen and set it to paper. Certainly I had something to say to you, dear cousin, of more moment than 'How are you enjoying life in Zurich?' or 'What was the weather like in Turin?'…I mentioned that my pen – the red one I always prefer to use – could not be found. Well, I must have been writing in bed last night (although I don't know what I can have been writing – an earlier draft of this letter perhaps?) for it has just turned up in my right – no, left slipper. It's hard to keep any sense of order or organisation in this place, though I *do* try – tying things in bundles, stacking them in neat piles, making complicated lists and attaching labels whenever it seems appropriate. Also I leave myself notes: this morning I found one in my dressing gown pocket; it said 'Remember the carnations. Recipes. String', and it makes no sense to me at all! I even bought a filing cabinet last month. Another bad idea, I'm afraid. Lost the key within a week and had to attack the thing with a hack-saw.

Somehow having a pen in one's hand helps to concentrate the mind, and now I remember why I had to write to you. I hope you've still got that spare room, the one with the view of the park and the church with columns, since I have decided to resign my position as official dwarf to the Duchy of Pluvia. Over the last couple of months there's been a lot of muttering in the palace. It amounts to this: people have been saying I'm not *short* enough. Well, I ask you!…The Chamberlain has been dropping heavy hints, remarking that since I am such a promising pianist why don't I take up *that* instead. And, truth to say, only the other week I performed a little *Valse-fantasie* of my own composition to great applause…But this is not the point. You of all people must be aware that from my earliest years I have been a dedicated dwarf. You will remember that wonderful birthday when we were all gathered in the family home, and I was presented with my first cap and bells, and at the moment the fir-tree was set on fire (according to our customs) the great knitted hanging – the work of poor, crazed Aunt Lydia – was unfolded showing in all its splendour the family tree – and in each generation a dwarf! You will remember how I tumbled down the stairs disguised as a marmoset, how I skipped about amid the dishes of the banqueting table, how I blew the toy trumpet astride the giant pine-apple, how the lights were turned out so I could climb up inside the sumptuous petticoats of the ladies without causing embarrassment. It's true I've grown a bit since then but not immoderately – why, I can still conceal myself under the cushions of the average sofa and leap out grimacing with all the artistry of a centuries-old tradition to frighten the children so they scream and vanish behind the numerous Japanese screens scattered about the palace to be found, hours later, still whimpering. This results in the most touching domestic scenes.

But how happy those early days were! You remember how I glued my father's wig to his head? Oh, he went to his grave still wearing it! It was the source of endless jokes and diversions. And let us not forget the time I danced on the puppy and broke its neck – such gaiety! Then, it all seemed to flow so easily. I was never short of ideas or delighted applause. But here, in Pluvia, things go from bad to worse. A miasma of forgetfulness infests everything, and it is only with the greatest difficulty that I resist the contagion. It can attack suddenly: in the streets of the capital it is not uncommon to see experienced cyclists suddenly waver and crash to the ground, expressions of utter astonishment on their faces. And only yesterday the state limousine simply rolled into the lake: now, because of its colour (a very pale silver-grey) no one can find it and the chauffeur, who was sleeping, is presumed dead. It was worse the time the head gaoler forgot where he had put his keys. For nights, for a week the whole town was kept awake with the howls of starving prisoners. No one could think what to do. When at last the keys were found, baked inside a loaf, it was too late for most of them: only a handful of dissident poets, scientists and musicians remained alive. Their accounts of the ordeal were published recently, each volumes long, exquisitely detailed and contradictory. Naturally a lavish state funeral was staged to appease the enraged relatives but at the grave-side the Archbishop couldn't remember a word of the service and the duchess began to snore while standing bolt upright in a position of embarrassing prominence.

Here it is common to confuse dreaming and waking – and fashionably one must affect to prefer the former. Even the language is beginning to alter. Everyone repeats everything, as if they were afraid of forgetting what they had said, or as if they had (indeed) forgotten that they had just said it. Even the meaning of words is affected: the word which last year meant 'forest' now means 'uncle', while the word 'edifice' signifies complex feelings of regret. So you can see there's little to keep an active spirit... Perhaps the Chamberlain has a point. I polish the phrases of my *Valse-mazurka*, my *Étude honteuse* and try to maintain a picturesque appearance. Tonight there's a gala performance for the Moroccan ambassador so it's back to the business of pretending to die of a broken heart while smiling bravely through tears, and once again

I dread the moment in any performance when it is time to laugh. Will they remember this time or will the usual muttering begin: 'How is it done? Ho, ho? Ha? Hee, hee? Ha, ho, ha?...

Please be so good as to place a monument on the flowers of my dead mother. Toss a well-stuffed cushion to the jaundiced hound. Derision and lashes to your delightful daughters. Tip the mood with a bushel of starlight for me, will you? Believe me you are rose to my puzzled cloud in longing and neuralgia. My blue pen turns sleepy.

Loaves and buskins,

Your Dwarf.

According to their Mythology

for Al Morgan

They were always chewing the leaves they collected at sunrise
and stored in small pots bearing simple, incised designs.

They had no work-ethic, which made things difficult when it came to
    draining the swamp,
and most of their jokes were serenely concerned with dying.

It was discovered that the hallucinations affected
only their perception of themselves. Sometimes
they saw themselves as tall giraffe-like creatures
and sometimes they were no higher than lap-dogs.
On tall days it was not uncommon for them to die of their
    extravagances, –
over-estimating their power and invulnerability
they would leap from cliff-tops, attack neighbouring tribes or
    government officials
who, naturally, were forced to respond. On small days

they became nervous and shy,
displaying a mania for collecting and storing
apparently useless objects, – old pieces of string, plastic whistles, cups

for picnics, soap-powder coupons...Often
they would hide for hours under beds or in cupboards.
In both states they proved capable of inventing songs:
tall songs addressed themselves to ancestors, flag-poles
and other worlds (of which, according to their mythology,
there were twelve); small songs
praised the hearth, the cooking pot and male children,
and it was these we were unable to record.

It was difficult to appreciate the usefulness of a habit
which, on occasion, seemed to threaten their very existence
but in the year the crop failed we saw in their faces
something very like despair, and we began to understand
their profound loathing of sobriety. So you will realise

how, at this crucial juncture, it is impossible for us
to return. Soon we will understand completely, –
our hands, our lips already stained a deep blue with the juice of the
      drug,
our tongues aching from the difficult languages of the twelve worlds.

But I can hardly speak. I feel
I am confined inside a drinking bowl.
I am, surely, the seed inside the smallest berry,
and if I were to say more you would not understand me.

Without Being Evening

*'No doubt the people of Priene...watched the Persians cutting
down their fruit trees, and followed with hopes and doubts the turns
of the day.'*

Freya Stark: *Ionia*

Concerning the crisis that is coming:
it happened yesterday. Meanwhile
we sit in cafés, and the music continues –
sentimental as ever, strewing roses in your lap...

We sit in cafés, on the steps
of the parliament building watching
small storms attack the encircling mountains:
the city is bound within a ring, a ring

thrown down in boredom. We sit still,
but for the eyes, the hands, the mouths –
their work is never done: they are sleepless.

The Church Of The Fallen Angel
is packed to the door. We would like to move

but are uncertain whether to choose
the forward or the backward path –
besides, we can no longer distinguish
between them. Who would risk a step?

If anyone walks a straight road
with a determined pace, that person
hasn't a thought in his head! And that is
why our women's waists are pulled in,

why flounces hamper them, why the bank
is entered through a rotunda,
why the great road goes round and round

and round the city, with the grand canal,
the tram lines, and oppressed infantry of trees –
it's a round-dance, a round-dance!

                *

Life is hidden away behind gothic arcades,
Medicean rustications, magnificent
uninhabitable loggias, funereal vestibules! . . .

Each person carries an invisible garland of stone –
even the newest apartments look ancestral,
full of shadows, ready to welcome their first ghosts.

Like a doubt in the mind of an autocrat
an oval of moonlight shifts
across the glassy floor of a stairwell,

and our dreams retreat from the horizon –
they go down, they reveal the enemy in our souls,
the daubed barbarian and an Asiatic melancholy...

But the idea of The End is utterly discredited
and the map of the city resembles
the cross-section of a tree-trunk or an onion.

*

Over there, they are building a tunnel for the river;
they are building tenements for the workers –
at a safe distance, close to the abattoir, the new barracks
and the mounds of the demolished Jewish quarter.

They are damming the mountain streams;
lakes for pleasure craft cover the ancient poverty of villages:
there will be no flood, no flood.

The nomads who, last year, encamped in the gardens
of the outlying villas have been driven out;
only their songs remain on the air –
cursive, like a script full of oaths and loathing.

*

The assassinated emperor disembarks
under a dome of glass and metal...

Steam! Violins! Majolica roses!
Oiled moustaches! Braided uniforms! Saliva and kisses!

A glistening machine, all cogs and chains
and wheels (and wheels within wheels)
hauls him to the highest balcony
and the concert begins –

Poor Mozart, poor Beethoven
you are left far behind primitive masters

your symphonies are vegetable patches or postcards
compared to these all-encompassing panoramas
swollen with tubas, bells, organs, anvils and gongs
and lasting for hours, lasting for whole evenings on end.

But something shivers, and trembles,
a shadow passes over the audience
the orchestra squeals faintly, groans and slithers into

silence...
and it is over before it began –
this evocation of the snow-storm
and lament for the dead mother:

then from the plush bourgeois
abyss
emerges hatred
with whistling and hisses!

      *

From café terraces it is pleasant to watch
the changing colours of the mountains
as evening approaches, to conjure
images of those near places it would be
too troubling actually to visit –

places where, at this hour, a deer steps down
to a blue pool like an eye that, now and then
blinks a little out of tiredness (it will never
be put out), or a feminine youth falls asleep

under the briars, dreaming of a knife
and a wolf's skin, and the leaf
in his clenched fist turns red...

The news is bad, but that is no reason
to alter the habits of a century; besides,
reports are confused: effects precede their

causes, there are resurrections and erasures –
deaths as never before, births as never before

and it is pleasant to watch the sunsets
with a critical and comparative eye –
their golds and mauves exceed the paintings
in exhibitions of the avant-garde:

it is pleasant ... but their intensity
unnerves like the gaze of a neurotic
from whom politeness forbids you to escape,
a gaze which reveals the desire for some
violent, meaningless action. Darkening

west, it is from you that rain clouds have come
to cut short our summer,
and the rose bushes, the nests are ruined
in the small garden where, only yesterday,

we celebrated the Infanta's birthday
with so many charming speeches
and the music of a piano trio.

The café tables are moved indoors, the chairs
piled crazily in towers at the corners
of the terraces, statues are boarded up
against the cold, and, urged by the wind

something approaches as a murderer
approaches the quiet, isolated house:

blown yellow leaves cling to the victim's eyes,
damp brown leaves seal his mouth.

Ghost Preludes

1

Too late to talk of moorings
or bed rock. The scent of mushrooms
or sorrel carries us far away:
an interminable drunken conversation
is the fate of exiles. Abrupt

melodies of extinct instruments
are transcribed at night. But who
has any use for them now –
the second thought and backward glance

towards the old homestead in the pines,
the ancestral cow, the children with voices
like randomly plucked banjo strings,
those pianos the peasants dumped in the pond?

It seems (a law) the speed of the vehicle
increases as the attractions
of the probable destination diminish –

by now it is a wretched, clapboard lodging-house
filled with the unvisited senile and demented:
indeed, it could move still further
from little to less to least –

white light and dust in which you and yours
are not. Meanwhile
it's best, so they say, to take up some hobby –
photographing hotel lobbies, knitting
slogans into cardigans . . . And the empty

spaces in the log book ache to be filled.
O memoirs, documentaries, mountainous journals!
the text is always and in all places
irretrievably corrupted. Did you think
you could just pick up language and use it,

as if it were a pen or a spade –
the one called *a spade?*...

Vast, desiccated tribes of scholars
mount doomed expeditions
into the wilderness of errata bordering

the boggy shores of frozen Lake Lacuna.

2

The project on which they all had laboured
in near poverty and star-like fervour
had to be abandoned: it was, perhaps,
only another example of that 'new architecture'
the public furiously rejects, smearing its stairwells
with obscenities, signatures and urine...

The friends departed under a drenching autumn shower
and soon news came that one had died by his own hand,
on others silence fell like a cowl. Still others
wrote proclaiming their happiness, but in the telling
it proved only a diminished contentment

like that of a child pressing to his flushed cheek
the soft shreds of a blanket or shawl, or else
it was no more than a fixed watching
for (say) yellow dahlias to appear
at the drab end of a short garden. Was all

in vain
then? Not all –

for some things assuredly stick in the mind
like parts of thistles in woollen trousers
after the blandness of a long country walk
(of the sort so many people are taking today
in hopes of forgetting the thing that once
so excited them repose was possible only in

stunned drunkenness). Like so much else
to do with politics or philosophy –
the questions of that time, intrusive as
an illuminated brand-name flashing
beyond the window of a hotel bedroom –

the past had been put in (the velvet
and dim columns in the back drop)
for purposes of recognition: who could forget
her song about the sound of his spurs
still ringing in the empty square
before the white palace foundering like a liner –

those mirrors you could enter or leave at will? ...
Much besides might be arrayed,
armada-like, under the banner 'Unforgettable' –
those statues casting shadows on the staircase,
the umbrellas massed before the massacre,
rainstorms pounding the desolate café tables ...

Why then were there lines of such a vacuous nobility
no one could shape them with any conviction?
It could be that too much work had been done in darkness,
or too many opiates and oriental maxims were swallowed
indiscriminately: harsh words, cruel acts
had so weakened the fabric of the world it was
equally difficult to believe our immediate responses
and would-be tranquil recollections. A blown fuse

threw the party into panic, the telephone rang
without ceasing, and in a corner
of the dismal room two thugs were pinning down
a perfect stranger who constantly protested
an innocence no one could believe. *O choir*
of earth and furniture of heaven!

the gulping music lied to us.

Street Musicians

for Tassos Denegris

There must be mountains
inside those clouds
and the sea still exists
where the port once was.

A bitter rain attacks
the last, Byzantine well-heads,
and the custodian eyes you suspiciously
as if you might steal that acanthus
fragment or postcard of a saint –
as if understanding were possession.

The town (this venerable city
on which so much love
and unmotivated loathing
has been squandered like spittle
or semen) the town is a book
which ill-disciplined teams of citizens
carry to the desk of the dying scholar
whose cry of understanding stays unwritten.

We are studying the forms
of responsibility, the burdens of the past
and when the plans for the new Acropolis
are unveiled votes will be cast
in the form of razor marks on plastic.

*

A cold wind invades a square
stocked with petrified social reformers,
scours those corners where the smoke
of fifty years ago still hopes to linger

and always one side of the square is missing –
the project was never completed
the buildings were recently demolished, always

black stains of the high windows' tears reach down
the sheer precinct walls, narrowing
to a paint-brush's point above
the ageing clarinettist's head.

And what tune
has he dragged out of his fond youth
(a tune such as he used
to whistle to his starved greyhound
or lovelorn pigeon on evenings
etched with rime) that he distorts it so
with lubricious slides and yelps, next
to the doorway of the smart-in-the-sense-of-derelict boutique?

O he casts such loathing glances towards
the long-haired girls playing their trio-sonata
in the shadow of the dispensing chemist's . . .

And who could blame him? Their music is torture,
so wilfully emphasising the decline
in ornament and architecture

that the ordinary action
of buying today's onions, today's cigarettes and gin
is invested with all the sadness
of an enlightened emperor's funeral

and even the punks emerging
empty-handed from the record store
in an armour of leather and metal
and brilliant hair shaped into knifeblades
are consumed with nostalgia
for the year '77. You might say –

'Their jeans are not more torn than my heart'
but, like a frazzled hairpiece, it won't convince.

It isn't hope that is betrayed
but its certain absence, so you must suffer
the repeated appearance of vague, smiling presences
in what had been an ideal vista of desolation.

*

No use lamenting the caryatid's faces
melting in the rain as if they were modelled in snow –
this is not Attica, Attica is not Attica,
or it is a prison. Plans for the new Acropolis
are well advanced. From that clear height
the mountains will be visible. We will identify

the place of the beehives,
the place of the fountain,
the place of cyclamen and plane trees,

and further off the sea flashing like a hero's shield
coloured as it was in the old verse narratives
will tell us the rumours are false
that its surface has not hardened and cracked
like the surface of a waterhole in the Sahel
and even the smallest boat with the most delicate
yellow sail can be taken out in safety.

Of course, there are problems
as I will admit and you will admit
since in the meantime we must try to live
clear of hunger and boredom,
and who would choose to be the trumpeter
cracking notes all day outside a crowded charcuterie?

But there is community in despised professions
and when the street musicians look down
into the deep red or blue linings of their instruments' cases
they are like divers, like archaeologists

discovering for the first time after centuries of burial,
centuries of invention and vast migrations no one understands,
a lost beauty, a vanished art like a living face –
Philip of Macedon's tomb.

The Lecture

A Professor expounds certain Ideas on the Nature of Crowds

As he knew – the American fountainhead – describing the crowd in the street of a modern city can be a difficult business, and it is reasonable to ask whether anyone has ever wholly succeeded in the task. One must proceed with caution, refusing to think of a crowd as an anonymous mass or collective organism – some impossible hydra-headed beast inimical to the life of the individual. After all, in any given crowd there may be many people with whom one could hold agreeable and instructive conversations simply by removing them from the street to a chair at your kitchen table.

We could begin our researches by isolating faces, gestures or even whole individuals from the crowd as it advances (perhaps in the morning from the direction of a station). For example, the shambling man who stops passersby to ask for money, or the office girl, neither ugly nor pretty, whose face is reflected in a wide shop window. But these figures must be dismissed: the first points in the direction of altruism or 'social concern', the second towards an easy pathos – shallow emotions powerless to effect in any way (still less transform, if only in words) the unsatisfactory reality of which these are weak examples. Besides, to begin with individuals, however typical we may imagine them to be, is to evade the issue. Instead let us imagine that a short stretch of pavement on a busy street is to be the subject of an experiment involving a new kind of camera which would record in a different colour the track of each passerby. These would overlap, swerve, intersect and double-back. They would reveal an intimate record of all the minute variations of movement, and momentary relationships between individuals in a defined space that can be said to constitute a crowd. Each track would be different from the next in some way but many would closely resemble each other. We could attach labels to the tracks: a blue line might be 'The Portly Businessman', a red line 'The Young Homosexual', a green line 'The Elegant Woman'... But I should stop here since these colours might be understood as *emblematic*, and individuals would be reduced in this way to the visible ghosts of ideas – conformity, rebellion, sexuality and so on. This might be permissible in some poetic allegory expounding the ways of God or fashionable economists, but would contradict and hopelessly obfuscate our present purposes. As we proceed we must guard against this tendency to symbolise which is so ineluctable, so irresistible to the human mind (even to minds very

93

developed) that it must be considered a vice which, perhaps, is responsible for many grave injustices.

Our experiment would have to be very limited in scope or it would fail – there would soon be no more colours left. It is, of course, a disheartening but irrefutable fact that the rainbow, once a divine messenger and portent, is soon exhausted, but this is a problem which will surely be solved before too long, for there can be no limit to possibility in a world where what was once unthinkable is an everyday occurrence, as my patient reader will be able to attest from his own experience. If, for the moment, we continue with the limited means at our disposal we will find ourselves driven to ever more subtle half-tones – grey-mauves, purple-pinks, milky blue-greens, opals and faded amber – and, gradually, our paradigm will become as obscure and blurred as a fogbound airport. This could be regarded only as an alteration of degree – a passage from a hard-edged to an impressionistic abstraction. We would then have to re-examine our reasons for undertaking the experiment. It may be that to regard this record of the crowd simply as a dense and satisfying abstract design, such as would receive plaudits in some fashionable gallery, will seem dehumanising, but it is accepted that all art involves a certain ruthlessness towards its materials and that the serious art of this century tends especially towards dehumanisation (see Ortega, Sontag), for this unarguably is, despite miracles of inventiveness and ingenuity, a desolate and desolating era in which monstrosities of thought and deed bloom so constantly (like those flowers of evil first imagined with such luxurious distaste in the hectic Paris of a crapulous despot) that one is amazed to look from the window of one's room and find that there are indeed many people in the street, that they move quite easily and naturally...which thought brings us, not without a certain concision and artistry, back to the over-mastering concern of our little talk – that phenomenon whose definition, whose vaguest shape still eludes us as the image of the Beloved eludes the romantic poet gazing upon Freudianly explicit chasms, torrents and crags, but he, as we know, only glosses the gross appetites he shares with the crowd he affects to disdain, and – it goes without saying – disdain, contempt, condescension, loathing, fear and suspicion are emotions we must discard utterly when approaching our subject...for what concerns us here is principally the urgent need to avoid the idle lapse into a sterile and destructive conflict between moral and aesthetic values: I must insist the conflict is false, for it is impossible and besides *unnecessary* to say which tells us more about the crowd – the precise diagram or the blurred abstract...but it is perhaps best, at this juncture, to *look* at

94

a crowd since I find, on glancing out of my window, that many people are hurrying home from cinemas, theatres and other places of vulgar entertainment, unaware or swinishly ignorant of the fact that their every movement may be fateful – that the brains of the drunken boy in the padded nylon jacket may be crushed by a passing taxi, that a girl may slip in a slick of vomit and break her hip. . . .

And here I must stop, for I feel that in the necessarily tentative foregoing remarks I have trespassed beyond that objectivity which is my proper sphere, and that, somehow, the indescribable colours of bodily fluids have invaded that white atmosphere before which Mallarmé abased himself in appalled adoration (only to find at the foot of the vertiginous wall a pot of rouge lying broken). In conclusion I must ask you – silent interlocutor, invisible auditor – to climb by whatever means – by stairs, by lifts, pulleys, ropes or ladders – to some high point and gaze down on the crowd moving in the streets of your city. Doesn't it resemble a swarm of cockroaches? Don't they resemble a host of angels, circled in blinding light, incongruously burdened with newspapers, books, briefcases and bags full of groceries? I offer these suggestions in a spirit of humility and, I trust, disinterested enquiry.

The Weather, or The English Requiem

Yes, there are earthquakes and eruptions
on the other side of the world.
The houses shake. The people prefer
to sleep in the streets, even in winter.

Now the storms, the heavy heat confirm
distance from the event is no protection –
besides you live in a country where half the population
are criminals or fools, all of them
staring through sealed windows at the vast
cataclysm that is *the weather*.

*

Outside
(below)

in the dull street
beside the dirty canal

no one, just now,
is killing anyone. Why not
we want to know?

       *

Yes, the sewers collapse,
we have potholes as in New York
and we love them incontinently.

The street is quiet. No one disturbs
the trees when they let fall
their leaves. This is a dream, I'm afraid

and the pavements (unpaved)
are swimming with darkness.

Hairline cracks appear
even in the beautiful autumn sky
supplied by the American conglomerate.

       *

And we want to know
what has been done
to prevent this meagre conclusion

like an alley
bordered with rusting corrugations?

       *

The charter is proclaimed –
to every man his ghetto.

The ordinance has gone out –
a new and higher value
has been placed on water

as the undiverted lava-stream
having devoured
a parade of shops and restaurants
begins to press
its tongue against your doorstep.

      *

Didn't we pay enough?
Didn't we build enough?
Didn't we worship the gods in their temples?
Didn't we die enough?
Didn't we lie down under the wheels?
Isn't our blood
in the mortar of those noble structures
you would now disperse
with the wave of a hand around which
a bracelet dances,
its pendants addressed to death
and the inscrutable stars
that govern us?

      *

Yes we also look at the sky.
At intervals it turns black.

We fall down drunk
in the gutters provided

and a light glistens on our tongues –
we become incapable of treason.

      *

We look at our hands.
They are veined and creased
like the aerial photograph of a continent.

There are salt deserts and great lakes,
valleys full of orchards and vines,
ancient cities that refuse to die...

See how the shadows shift over them,
innocent shadows of beech leaves.

Isn't that also a betrayal?
A bird scuds low against the light
casting its vote for evening.

Desert Song

And so, as in the opening of a *quasida*
I address the remains of a campfire, –

the one we shared in the waterless outer precincts
of the riot-torn city...Beloved! O
moon among flickering lanterns, I am on my way, –

my light skiff negotiates with ease
the rusting hulks and gun-boats of the port,

and soon I am well advanced along the Grand Canal,
passing the Green Mosque,
skirting the Tower Of The Winds until

I disembark at the Square Of The Souks, –
famed in history and travelogue...

And here is something to mock the visitor,
for at the centre of the square lies
a massive compass-star drawn in white mosaic
on a ground of dull, red stone, –

and a compass is what you will need
(and of course you didn't think to bring one)
for it is easy to lose your way in this place

amidst the din
of metal workers and public address systems,
amidst the scent of grilling meats and burning charcoal,

among the roses and grottoes of the Monteverdi Gardens,
in the sound of rebecs, ouds, tramcars, telephones,
cavalry, and shells exploding along the besieged corniche!

Here are numberless distractions and alarms:
sometimes a man swaying under the weight of a fluttering totem
of lottery tickets will fall at your feet, smiling

as if death, or a woman with a scar across her throat
will call out confused words from the dim porch of an alley
(and she, you at once recognise, is a visitant
from another poem, not this one you are living)

– indeed, in no other city is panic so likely
to attack the stranger, and yet considerations
of religious taboo and military strategy
forbid the publication of maps. But courage,

oh my star! for I am still on my way,
clutching grimly at my water-flask, eyes fixed
on the exposed mechanism of the casino's clock tower, –

which is like our hearts, like the rich and complex feelings
that should be coming into play at this moment, amidst
the striking of bells and the ululations of muezzins,

if only I could find you. But, as is inevitable,
the sky begins to darken as if an immense shutter were sliding into place,
a fog rises from the canals and a swarm of starving people
stumbles through the narrow streets.

I am thrown aside into the crumbling pavilion
of a disused public fountain, and fear,
like a line of ants begins to crawl up my spine.

Malicious birds, carriers of disease, have devoured the crumbs I left as
        a trail,
and examination of my pockets reveals that I carry
no note of your address. The crowd thickens

and begins to chant in unison words
my phrase book does not record; they begin to lacerate their faces
with their nails; they begin to strike out at one another
confusedly with branches.
I dare not emerge from my hiding place,
and I am still on my way. Forever now.

The Road to Ogalma

Perhaps this is not a good day for you. A menacing letter has arrived
from the Ministry of the Interior. A lover, a wife or a husband has
phoned you with a voice full of hate. Alas, the small boat of your life is
about to capsize and the sharks are circling greedily. And you know that
this is the day that you must find Ogalma... If this is indeed such a day,
here is what you must do. You must leave the city very early in the morning, taking care that no policemen follow you. You must carry a stone
and a long stick in case you should meet some wild dogs. You must head
north, keeping the peak of Rose-Coco Mountain always in sight. At the
first cross-roads you will find a goat standing in the back of a broken-
down truck. Walk quickly past it, still heading for the north, until you
come across a man urinating in a field of maize. As soon as you see him
shout a hearty greeting (but do not on any account mention Ogalma)
and turn immediately to your left before he has a chance to reply. At first
you will find yourself in a savannah scattered with clumps of thorn
bushes, but soon you will come upon flowers. They are orange with
reddish-brown spots. You must pick some of these. Now it will begin to
rain and you should shelter under the branches of the nearest carob
tree. When the rain stops a cat will appear. Follow it along the path
between the tall bamboos. Voices will come from beyond the bamboos
– the voices of children, perhaps of your childhood friends, but you
must ignore them for the cat will not wait. He will lead you to a grotto
built of old petrol cans. This is the shrine of Mama Luza, patron of
drunkards. Leave your flowers but do not drink from the spring. You
must hurry for the shadows are lengthening. Ahead of you stands a row
of six prickly pear trees. You must pass to the right of the fourth tree
from the left and walk in a straight line until you come to a low shack,
roofed with old Pepsi-Cola signs. On the steps of the shack you will find
an old woman chopping yams with a big knife. When she sees you, you

should call out, 'Well, sister, did you dream last night?' and she will reply, 'Sit down and I will tell you.' If her dream is a dream of water and sky you need not worry, but if her dream is a dream of fire and blood you must beware. She will offer you a bed for the night and you are forced to accept since it is now quite dark and there is no moon in sight. Also you can hear wild dogs howling not far off. If she has dreamt of water and the sky you may sleep, but if she has dreamt of fire and blood you must stay awake all night, for it is possible that she will attack you with her knife. Pretend to sleep. If she creeps into your room holding the knife you need only sit up suddenly and stare at her without fear. She will scurry away like a spider, whimpering and cursing to herself. In the morning you must behave as if nothing has happened. You will find her scattering grain for her hens, but amid the hens a very beautiful hoopoe will appear. Before it has eaten very much the hens will drive it off. Be quick now, you must follow it. You must run down a hill through a banana plantation. Then you must jump over a stream on the far side of which there is a flight of steps overgrown with moss. Run up the steps. At the top the hoopoe will alight on a broken statue. The head of the statue is missing and vines have ensnared it, but it is still possible to tell that it represents a naked woman carrying a sheaf of arrows. You must imagine the head of the woman; you must imagine her eyes and estimate the direction they must once have looked in. Now walk in that direction and you will come upon a great house. It is the house of a rich man who was killed by his slaves in the Great Rebellion. Now you are very near Ogalma. Approach the house with an air of nonchalance. Do not believe the tales of vampires that are told about this place. It is certain that the last vampire packed up and left for Europe more than thirty years ago. There *are* ghosts of course but it is too early in the day for them to bother you. Enter by the central door. You will find yourself in a room with many pillars, its floor scattered with bat droppings, dead leaves and broken glass pendants. Walk quickly to the far end of this room looking neither to right nor left, but be careful, – the floor is slippery. You will find a small doorway half-hidden by ferns and beyond it a narrow passage in which a poisonous fungus grows in shapes like thunder clouds and dripping candle-wax. Step carefully and try to hold your breath for the air is full of fungus spores which may cause nausea and dizziness. If you should faint here you may never reach Ogalma, but have courage, the passage is short and at its end you will emerge on to a broad sunlit terrace. Below you lies a valley in which many plantains grow. And rising from the valley you will see a column of pure white smoke. It is the smoke rising from the giant spliff of Ogalma. You will find him resting in a hammock. Do not disturb him. After a time he will notice you. He will say: 'So you are here at last. You must be a very clever man. How did you manage to find me?' And you must reply –

'I left the city in the early morning when the shadows were still long. No police followed me. I carried a stone and a long stick. I walked towards the peak of Rose-Coco Mountain. At the first cross-roads I came upon a goat standing in the back of a broken-down truck, but I walked quickly past it and continued towards the north until I saw an old man urinating in a field of maize. I called out loudly, "A good year for the crops, brother!" but before he could reply I turned to the west and began to cross a savannah of thorn bushes. Soon I came upon some flowers. They were white with red stripes. As I bent down to pick them it began to rain so I took shelter under the branches of a nearby carob. The tree was low so I had to crouch. Ants crawled around my feet. When the rain stopped a handsome grey cat appeared and I followed it. It led me along a narrow path between tall bamboos. Voices of children came from beyond the bamboos and I remembered a summer many years ago when I went with my brothers, my sisters and my cousins to the big river near our village; I remembered the cool water on my feet and the taste of the mangoes we had picked on our way...I must have stopped for a few seconds. Perhaps I closed my eyes, for suddenly the cat was gone. I ran to the end of the path and stumbled into a car cemetery. There was no sign of the cat. A mound of Mercedes, Chevrolets, Buicks, Toyotas and Volkswagens was surmounted by a crumpled Cadillac. Beyond the cars I saw the prickly pears. I passed to the right of the fourth tree from the left and walked in a straight line until I came across an old woman chopping yams in front of a low shack. I called out to her "Well sister did you dream last night?" and she replied, "Sit down and I will tell you." I offered her the flowers which she accepted. This was her dream. "I was floating on a great calm ocean. My skirts billowed like the sails of a galleon. All around me my good friends were also floating. We exchanged greetings, quite naturally as if we had met on our way to a market. A breeze carried us on over the water which was clear as glass. The fins of a small fish brushed against my legs. Not far off I heard the deep laugh of my friend Syreeta who is very ticklish. After some time I saw that we were approaching land and I heard bells ringing. The breeze shifted and the whole fleet of women rounded a cape. Before us was the most beautiful city I have ever seen. There were walls of white stone, roofs of gold and windows of green glass. Many flags fluttered above the roofs, the streets were carpeted with roses and all the people of the city were running in the direction of the harbour, pointing towards us, shouting – 'It is the Promised Ships, the Magic

Fleet! They have come to take us away from this dreadful place!' And I did not understand them for I was thinking that I would like to have lived in that city for the rest of my life. That was my dream." She smiled almost shyly. It was getting dark so I asked her if she had a place where I could sleep. She showed me to a room hardly bigger than a cupboard, but it was clean and the bed was soft. I spent a peaceful night. Roosters woke me. In the yard I found red hens pecking at grain. But in their midst was a bird of a kind I had never seen before. About the size of a pigeon, it was very graceful; its high crest was the blue of irises, for the rest it was coloured a dusty pink with crescents of pale grey on its wings. I asked the woman the name of the bird. She said only: "It is your bird." At this the hens began to attack the bird and it flew off. I ran after it, down a hill, over a stream and up a flight of steps. (I did not stop to think what a flight of steps was doing in this place.) The bird alighted at the foot of a white statue. The statue had no head and lacked an arm but I saw that it had been the statue of a women, even though the breasts were also mutilated. I thought of her head and her eyes. And her eyes appeared before me and I saw which way they looked. I began to walk slowly along the line of her gaze which led me through a shallow pond, a thick hedge and into an open field. At once I saw the magnificent ruins of a house built of yellow stone with many columns and a hundred dark windows. Then from the windows and from between the columns wild dogs ran out howling like ghosts and baring their teeth. I remembered my stone. I threw it. I swung my stick in a wide circle and I cursed the race of dogs. And this I do not understand, for they fled away without more ado. They seemed horrified and ashamed as if I had broken some unspoken understanding. Now I could approach the house, and I began to tremble – surely this must be the home of vampires. I thought of their glistening lips, their pale skin, elegant gestures and soft speech. But I walked to the central door and entered. I found nothing, only a vast space littered with torn books and broken wine-bottles, some pools of water and weeping ferns. At the far end of this space I saw the opening of a narrow corridor. This I also entered feeling very pleased at my fearlessness. But I must say, Ogalma, that I was very foolish, for the corridor was almost blocked with strange plants in the shapes of deformed children, withered breasts, snarling mouths, leprous hands. I began to feel very dizzy. Suddenly my mother appeared shouting why didn't I eat the plants since I hadn't eaten for a day and a half. "You think you can live this way?" she screamed, "Stupid, bad, wicked boy. Why did you go away?" Then she shrank away and vanished. Next my father appeared, enraged and drunk. He grew very tall and vomited as if he would never stop. I fell down drenched and suffocated. I think

I fainted. After a time I felt a child's hand tugging at my sleeve, though no child was present. I saw that sunlight was pouring into the corridor and I crawled towards it. I saw, briefly, a priest, a policeman and an American soldier, but the light passed through them and I laughed. I laughed for a long time, moving slowly towards the light. This is why my hands are scarred and why my knees bleed, Ogalma. From the terrace I looked down with joy to see the white smoke rising from your giant spliff. And so I came to you and waited.'

Then Ogalma will say –
'Yes, this is very good, but what happened next?'
And you must say –
'Then Ogalma said to me, "So you are here at last. You must be a very clever man. How did you manage to find me?"'
And Ogalma will say –
'And how did you reply?'
And you will say –
'I told him how I left the city early in the morning before the sun had risen, how no one saw me, how I kept the peak of Rose-Coco Mountain always in sight, how at the first cross-roads I found a goat standing in the back of a broken-down truck, how I ignored the goat and the truck and continued to walk in a northwards direction, how I saw an old man pissing in his field of maize and turned immediately to the left, how I came upon flowers with trumpet mouths, how the rain fell and where I sheltered, how the cat appeared, what the old woman told me of her dreams – her fleet of women, her beautiful city whose inhabitants desperately desired to leave it.'

And you will pause. Your voice will falter, and you will say, 'But you are not Ogalma.' And he will smile in mockery and forgiveness.

104

Part Two: New York

from **Disbelief**

Unwilling Suspension

The cab should take off at this point
climbing straight over the river like a gull.
You can get so far but no nearer.
The island may be mirage or projection:
its towers remain on the horizon, –
the work of an ambitious child with scissors.
The bridges haven't been built, or they are
pitifully few. The roadway moans.

This is not The Good Place
and it assuredly is. In the evening
the sun makes it a glory
and deep in fissures, under fire-escapes,
are people who go hungry
and they seem to complain so little
they might be saints who had chosen
this way. Why have you come here?
It will not bring comfort, –
if you want that look somewhere else,
in the pages of an album or the far reaches of a park.

With oaths and hand gestures
the route changes: we shift north
passing between subsiding warehouses,
under obscure constructions of rusted girders,
discovering isolated houses with floral balconies,
carved doorframes. For some time we watch
elevators rising and falling in a distant building.

There needs to be a new religion of the city, –
a bible only of long-lined psalms
for long-lined buildings and their lights.

People sleep on the vents.
At night fireflies buzz the towers.
But we aren't getting any nearer
and how can I tell you how it feels
to spend an hour advancing by inches toward
something resembling a faded, theatrical curtain?

How can I tell you? The legends accumulate
like wealth or grain at the edge of a famine.
You will never be bored and you will never
conclude your investigations since the crime
has no culprit, or too many to fit in the old courthouse.

The cab stalls on the far bank, its headlights ablaze.
I couldn't photograph any of this for you.
I couldn't show its reflection in a windshield.
I could tell you about the rain: it is not raining.

Memories of Italy

I loved the light of course
and the way the young men
flirted with each other.
I loved the light, –

the way it fell out of a sky like a painting,
or perhaps like the ground (if this
is not too paradoxical a way of
putting it) for a painting,

and the way the young men stood in the station
wearing jeans that were the colour of the sky
or the sea in a painting, jeans that revealed
the shapes of their legs which reminded me

of the statues in the square outside the station
where the light fell with such violence
their shadows were blacker than the despair of the painter
who cannot proceed with the painting: the canvas
is before him, its ground blue and blank as the sky above the station

where the young men loiter like the heroes in one of the lulls of the
    Trojan War
when lazy picnics were possible beside the calm sea, under the smiling
    sky,
and it half seems that the war will end forever, for surely they must all
    soon fall in love with each other...
And the painter knows his painting must be heroic, that the blue is not
    the sky
but a terrible sea a God has raised to drown the beauty of the young
    men in the marble battlefield of the station,

and he knows the painting is finished,
that it represents the envy the divine must feel
towards the human as marble must envy the sea,

and the painting is hung in the concourse of the station
and the young men drift indifferently to and fro before it:
their feet hardly seem to touch the blue marble ground.

The Other Great Composers

They lived in places tourists don't care to visit
beside streams the obscure workings of local pride
insisted were rivers: there were willows or derelict mills
sometimes a boathouse with Palladian ambitions, –
in the backwoods, except that the towering pines were
often as not, replaced by clusters of factory chimneys, –
isolate, the factories gone, the chimneys octagonal,
grand as columns remembering a Trajan victory
although severely unadorned. They lived in places where
commerce destroyed the Roman forts, the common fields
with red viaducts, canals now, like them, disused

and forgotten, depositories for ignorance, or else
they sank into the confines of a half-suburban dream
of pastoral they couldn't share: the works grew longer,
'unperformable'...The aggression of the ordinary,
the tepid love expressed in summerhouses too small
really to contain lover and beloved, the muted modes
and folksongs rediscovered, dead as elms, drove them
to new forms of learning and excess, ruthless
distortions of the academic tones and tomes,
chords that decayed over long bars into distances
where bell-hung, bird-haunted pagodas of their own
design rose up, tier on tier, to radiant mountains, –
mountains from which they confidently expected,
year after year, the arrival of the ancient and youthful
messenger who would confirm the truth of these visions.
It is impossible yet to say that they were wrong:
the music is unproved and undisproved; their operas
require cathedrals in which the angels and grotesques
come alive for one scene only; their fugues and toccatas
demand the emergence of a pianist eight-handed
like a Hindu god whose temples remain a sheaf of sketches,
whose religion is confined to a single head, maddened
or happy, dead-centred in a continent of neglect.

The House Comes to Rest in its Garden

for Darragh Park

Sitting on the back porch with the painter and his dog
you remark the absence of car-alarms or voices yelling in Spanish,
then later find your sleep disturbed
by the stentorian exchanges of bullfrogs: yes,
the pond is inhabited and not so natural as it looks.

After nine months freezing and stewing in the city
you could make a fool of yourself out here. You might say –
'How perfectly the house fits its setting, how it seems
to snuggle down into its hillock like a dog into a sofa –
why, it seems to have grown up out of the place
like its graceful neighbour, the butternut tree! ...'

And how wrong you'd be! The whole house
was ordered in 1912 from *Sears & Roebuck*,
one of how many hundred editions of the same design,
and delivered in numbered parts by train. And it is hard

to imagine the distant town, clamped down under the rain,
where the walls and the windows, the roofs and the doors
were made, or their long, crated journey and the hurried assembly.

In those days people didn't just ship their houses out to the island,
they shipped their winter lives out into the summer,
bringing fat armchairs, elaborate drapes, classic libraries
and pianos no one played much, as little inclined
to accommodate themselves to the heat as Viceroys in the tropics,
and yet it was sea breezes that drew them from the city.

Are you disappointed by what you have learnt,
disappointed to find the marks of artifice and industry
where you expected nature? Not really,
for this unexpected information enhances, rather than spoils
your first grateful response to the sight of so many
different kinds of green surrounding an oval mirror of water,
and the garden, too, is a work of art that conceals art.

It looks almost wild, or at least like an uncropped field,
until you notice the new plantings which will compose themselves,
at the right season, into careful designs of pale blues and yellows,
purples and the pink of swamp-roses. It will be lovely.
It *is* lovely. An elliptical enclosure
of privet and honeysuckle (both now in pungent flower)
widely surrounds the butternut's swooping branches,
and you don't feel enclosed in any crowding sense
for gaps have been left in the hedge
through which a mass of chrome-yellow flowers will show,
and even on days when it is clouded or raining

sunlight will seem to fall steadily there –
a promise it would be too harsh to call false.

Croissant Outlets in Seattle

*'...je suis dévoué à un trouble nouveau, – j'attends
devenir un très mechant fou'*

There are still more hairs on my head
than there are croissant outlets in Seattle.
People tell me I'm looking good, but should I believe them?
Is anyone more trustworthy than a newspaper?

The tour of inspection has begun –
how exhausting it is –
and many there are who come seeking favours.
The reports pile up and the figures muddle me.

I feel childish but refuse assistance:
the last malfunctioning latrine must be registered.

In the dispiriting afternoons of these parts
I retire to the sheds behind the house
to work on the system I have devised which,
in time, will flood with unbearable light
the face of the nation: those wattled jowls

that still refuse to register, in even
the lowest key, one true emotion.

There are many now in minks who will be
exiled, perhaps to the Aleutians.

Ah bays and bridges! Towns, tunnels, ghettoes and gulfs!
Delicatessens and corporate headquarters!
Volcanoes, phonebooths and parking lots!
You will not escape my hand.

Is a tower of evil less evil because night
covers it with diamonds? Beautiful cankers
you will seem more like a poem
when I am through: you will be perfect roses,
innocent as the first day, installed
at all points of the city, like fountains
in the Turkish city of Bursa.

But it is too much for one man to do,
even if he had a good woman behind him,
and this is not the nineteenth century
of novels and puddings, of novels *like* puddings...

I regard the world as a TV
on which I change channels at will,
never moving from the bed:
everything must be in the place
where I can stare it in the face.
And I can't bear
for anyone to run
her fingers through my hair.

I will abolish the boudoir and the changing room;
there will be no more evening dresses or perfume!

Today the Union of the Mothers of Seattle
came bearing a petition, and they cried, –

'Oh save us! Install a priest as governor!
For the world seems to unravel like skirts
about our feet. The bread we buy is stale,
even before it leaves the store,
and good tomato paste cannot be discovered
anywhere in the state. Therefore
we come bearing a large cheque
which is yours if you will only
dispel this state of uncertainty

like the mist that never lifts from the summits
of our city's over-reaching towers.
Oh our city, lying beside its beautiful,
uninscribed pages of water and light!
Indeed we are littered like dry grasses
amid the play of water and light,
so, in our extremity, we come to you
with withered hands...'

Ah Seattle, Seattle,
with your boats and bridges and spires,
and your charming spruces,
I imagine you are like Norway.
You *will* be like Norway.

Already I see your vertiginous fiords,
the wooden houses of Bergen,
the profound dramas of your meagre households,
and over all is the pervasive odour
of herrings. But there remains
the matter of revising the folksongs.

A Lithuanian Mantilla

The night is clear.
The cows are in the byres.
The books are bound in quires.
Great stars appear,
and in the city of a hundred tottering spires
they are lighting festal fires, –
they are stringing lights on wires
all across the central square
and no one tires of this affair, –
the chance to vent suppressed desires
in huge chaotic choirs.

But dark mists rise from mires
in fetid corners of the shires
and men whom no man hires
fume with fury and despair
declaring: 'It's unfair, –
though each of us aspires
to sing a sweeter air
to shame the mansions of the squires,
how can we go dancing in the square
with no better prospect near

114

than dumbly sitting here?
For us these fires
bring no more cheer
than funeral pyres.'

The city walls are sheer,
the flames like spires,
and the people dancing there
have immolated fear:
their lying bards are bashing lyres.
This crowd acquires
only good news from the town criers.

In his high chamber the Emir
prances under a chandelier
with the wife that he admires
more than marriage quite requires.

Beyond the gates in darkness drear
a foppish cavalier
is caught in tangled briars.
Underneath the moonlight's glare
lines of masochistic friars
wander in an atmosphere
dismal as towns in Delaware.
Vast herds of deer. The stars austere.
Buildings designed by Albert Speer.

And the people in the square
declare: 'We are debonair,
each one of us a millionaire.
Beneath these splendid portières
we dance untouched by fear or care.'
They are not liars,
but people warmed by festal fires
rarely think of what transpires
when sunlight burnishes the spires:
the dancer tires
and every fire expires.

Men, Women, and Children

for my brother Nicholas

Say that life is a festive marching to no purpose
other than to assert that we are all here
with the old jokes and 'deviations from the norm',
the embroidered Union-banners of self, –
that the silence which falls on us unexpectedly
is the shimmering silence of a theatre foyer
while the performance is in progress,

and it seems some quiet, backwoods drama
of upright pianos and reticent avowals is involved...
but the spectacle, with all its noise and patent
absurdity is 'in our blood', and as the march continues
we meet friends and strangers with flashing smiles:
there is a band and the singing is defiant
but with a tendency to break up into laughter
as a wave shatters into diamonds, until

we are forced to think of our destination, –
the oppressive portals of the capitol,
the altars still smelling of blood.

Soul Music

Like the young
Aretha Franklin

the boy looked at his feet,
needlessly ashamed.

Imagined applause
thundered down streets

like crevices in crumbling brickwork,
and the real bricks crumbled,
the stones were losing their shape, –

stones of the doorway,
stones of the stairway,
stones of the lintel and the arch...

Perhaps the city would soon drain away
into the canals, the rivers and the sea
that daily sent its gulls to remind him
of its coldness and its closeness?

There was no kindness in the man sprawled
in the hallway, singing like a saw,
his one bandaged leg blocking all passage.

He was only looking for a home of some kind
but couldn't find it anywhere on the maps
the city authorities had set up in bus shelters.

At the excavations they discovered
a shopping precinct under the shopping precinct.

To his father
the sports pages were scripture
to which he offered the incense of a foul
tobacco; his mother sang to him, –
old songs of a reduced inheritance

Nothing said live,
nothing said hope, –

so the boy was lost for many years
and no one could trace him
even in landscapes constructed out of music,

until a voice, summoning
slandered histories, sprang out
like a tree from which the wind
stripped petals without depletion.

Surface Reversal

It is night and you are inevitably confused,
having travelled underground,

but now you're happy to find yourself
among the illuminated fountains and young trees.

The city is like a ballade
some people are singing on a bridge,   \

The wind is a hand pulling back sheet after sheet, –
all black silk, – from the cool bed of the river:

no one sleeps there, so we're told,
but somewhere the linen is heaped or folded.

Dim lights show on a barge
moored against the far quay,

and very obviously this is not a boat
but someone's memory of their lover who died.

The river flows to the west, the wind pulls to the east.
The cathedral dips its fan in both.

The Sudden Ending of Their Dream

The sudden ending of their dream
came when the wall collapsed
and they saw the water-wheel stop turning.
Something like a dust-cloud, but hunched
like an animal, rushed towards them.
They could no longer hear their neighbour
at his piano, and the birds
seemed to drop like stones. So they began again
outfacing what menaced their association.
Whose business was it but theirs? Not

history's or time's. The police were not watching them
although their vans rushed past hissing in the rain,
and black princesses sheltered nervously in doorways.

They began again, –
under the chestnuts in flower, on the bridges,
under the marvellous clouds, beside the statues.
If anything could be saved they would save it.
If life was empty they would bring food and flowers,
wine and illustrated books.
They staggered home in the evenings
carrying bread and enormous newspapers,
still thinking of the bronze head
they had seen in the museum. Light flashed
from the rim of a lunette. Storms of laughter passed over them
A party was always going on in the courtyard below,
and as the wall began to crack behind them
they studied the plans for the kiosk they would build.
It was the old urge not to be shut out of heaven,
not to shut heaven out. The sky kissed their hands.

The Sky My Husband

The sky my husband
The sky my wife
The sky my country and my grief
The sky my courtyard and my fountain
The sky my hyacinth
The sky my flock of birds and my guitar
The sky my kitchen and my knives
The sky my winter coat my summer shirt
The sky my balloon my acrobat
The sky my dancing-floor
The sky my café and my cinema
The sky my park and my path between the statues
The sky my garden of white trees
The sky my carousel
The sky my opera and my madrigal

The sky my actors and my theatre
The sky my wind-mill
The sky my evenings and my books
The sky my taxi my *tabac*
The sky my attic my hotel
The sky my railways and my stations
The sky my cities and my stones
The sky my head my hair my limbs
The sky my eyes my spectacles
The sky my nights my neon
The sky my balcony my garland and my mask
The sky my terrace and my tables
The sky my avenues and bridges
The sky my chandelier my Chinese lantern
The sky my roots and branches
The sky my awnings and my hope
The sky my gulfs my lakes my canyons
The sky my arches and my aqueducts in ruins
The sky my waning moon my child
The sky my rivers and cascades
The sky my forests and my solitude
The sky my castle and my flight of stairs
The sky my windows and my roofs
The sky my aerials and factory chimneys
The sky my pavilion and my tomb
The sky my incense and my hymn
The sky my journals and my magazines
The sky my violin my piano
The sky my medals and my coins
The sky my puddles and my dust
Le ciel mes feux d'artifice
The sky my scarves my hats my gloves
The sky my showers my snow my salt my sleet
The sky my mansions and my mother
The sky my diary and my photographs
The sky my cedars and my roses
The sky my face my cake of soap
The sky my memory my mountains
The sky my paper boat my autumns and my loss
The sky my palms and my Sahara
The sky my porches and my atriums
The sky my galleries my icons

The sky my radio my satellite my video
The sky my drought my famine
The sky my street-lamps my alleys and my crowds
The sky my armies and my guns my death
The sky my exile and my winters
The sky my victories and massacres
The sky my ministries my lies my parliament my eloquence
The sky my labyrinth my irony
The sky my carnation my buttonhole my bed
The sky my rondos and my boredom
The sky my flotillas and my rafts of flowers
The sky my love-affairs my comedies
The sky my theories and forgetfulness
The sky my Paris my New York my Rome
The sky great wheel of lights and colours
The sky my Venice my Vienna and my Petersburg
The sky my Alexandria
The sky my empire my provinces my people
The sky my islands and my harbours
The sky my lullaby
The sky my blood my breath my home
The sky my end

The Hotel Brown Poems

1

Above every seaward-facing window
of the Hotel Brown is a canopy. At night
the perfumes of the garden will delight you...

It is a good place to fall in love
and a good place to write, though neither
is obligatory. You must, however,

praise the light, the changing colours
of the sea at dawn and dusk: these are
the divinities of the place. Amen.

2

Once in the cool, blue restaurant
of the Hotel Brown a friend said to me, –
'You don't realise how much your openness
frightens people: it hits them like a wave,'

and I smiled, not because his words
amused me, but because the scent of peppers
grilling in the kitchen overwhelmed me.
I could not think of ideas or people then –

only of the place, the scent, the way
long white curtains moved back and forth
across the boundaries of light and air.

3

The windows were open on to the small terrace.
the sea was motionless. Not a wave. I would not,
for the world, compare it to anything.

I pointed down the half-deserted quay
drowsy with a heat that seemed personal
like a memory, and said, 'That man, hunched

as if he were struggling against
a cold wind, is a poet, a friend of mine.
let's make ourselves known.'

4

Think of yourself as a wave. Hard.
Think of yourself as open. Equally hard.
Usually your gestures seem to take place
behind a glass partition, fogged with steam

and there is often the sense that things are closing in, –
have closed over you like the waters of a lamentation,
and the absence of obvious locks or bars only confirms
that depressingly, the fault lies in your soul as much

as hostile circumstances, the invisible clouds
of general despondency that hang off even the most
blissful shore, waiting to blow in, dulling
the water, the boats, your deepest words with dust.

5

As we walked towards the temple
the poet said to us: 'This may seem
a small island to you but once it was
an independent state with its own fierce navy.

The Athenians destroyed it utterly.'
The old ramparts were massive, finely jointed
but the area of jumbled stones and bushes they enclosed
seemed no bigger than a modest public park.

6

We saw him to the evening boat. A man
who walked like a dancer followed him aboard
carrying a single bicycle wheel, and the ship
departed, illuminated, unreasonably festive.

We walked back past the bars. The night
was already richly dark, full of murmured conversation.
Light poured down the steps of the Hotel Brown,
traversed by a cold, rising breeze, as if to say –

'You are welcome, for the moment. This
is an interval in your life. Soon you must look to
the plots and masks and backdrops of your next act.
Here all moments are intervals. It is like music and like loss.'

Unsentimental Journey

We see the envelope they are
but the soul of things stays shut
like a library on Sundays.

This is a remote provincial city
in a country you are visiting
for the first time. Who could believe
the depth of the dust covering the trees,
the numbers of burial mounds on the outskirts,
the hamburger joints punctuating the ancient streets?

The more precise the investigation,
the more the 'unknown quantities' multiply,
but it isn't the number of books
or paintings that exist in the world
of which we wished to be assured,
but their quality and veracity, –

the quality also of private impressions,
sudden recalls, customs and performances,
whether these should be set down in one form
or another, or allowed to decay
like towers of unbaked brick.

The rigour you may once have desired
is ruled out, for the objects are
attentive as the dogs in fables,
Ulysses' dog he had to kill, –

and an iridescence like the oil
spilt from gardening machinery
along cemetery walks after the rain
covers the remembered faces:
a good effect, but a puzzling one...

So much wants to exist, –
the echoing station you departed from,
the sandwich wrappers on the train,

the narrow hotel room with its view
of an open-air cinema's blank screen,
besides all the cities of Europe and America...

and when, in a very distant place,
a raised hand releases pennants of blood
you must orchestrate the outcry.

You have suddenly moved in from the margins,
and though you can't say how,
your response will be decisive like a battle
changing the allegiance and religion of a people.

But the most violent actions, the black howls
leave no trace, only an open field
with ruts and hillocks, a fence of trees.

From Lorca's Letters

The world is a shoulder of dark meat –
black flesh of an old mule –
and the light is on the other side
where there are sonorous spikes of wheat
and white processionals of clouds.

I embrace you and the horizon rises,
constructed like a great aqueduct,
and amid the chalk roses and canna-lilies of Egypt
the city of Alexandria raises towers
like stems of crystal and reddish salt.

The first snows have fallen. The yellow begins,
infinite and deep, to play with twenty shades of blue.

*

Since the weather is mild
the young ladies of Granada
climb to the whitewashed terraces
to look at the mountains.
(They do not look at the sea.)

The blondes go out in the sun.
The brunettes stay in the shade.

Those with chestnut hair remain in first-floor rooms
looking into mirrors, adjusting little celluloid combs.

And you will wet your braids in the sea
while the stuttering song of the motor-boats comes and goes,
and when you stand in the doorway of your house
sunset will light up the coral that the virgin holds in her hands.

How quiet it is! Only the stuffed bear
keeps you company. The maid has gone to the dance.

But now, for you alone, the two black dancers,
dressed in green and white crystal, will dance
the sacred dance of the windows and the door.

Memory sits in an armchair
eating cakes, drinking dark wine.
Under the white porticoes
an accordion is heard.

                    *

Here are some postage stamps
I have unearthed from your favourite century.

I don't know, Melchorito,
who these respectable gentlemen might be.

They seem to be musicians. *Are* they musicians?
Surely these are nights of Italian opera
and snow-covered roof-tops? Voices like diamonds
and fountains, orchestras of vaporous silk...

The young man in his heavy overcoat,
half a Roman and half a professor of literature,
must have died young, I think: consider his smile.

And the young woman looking through her glasses,
for a closer view of the handsome tenor,
doesn't wear a white crinoline
as some, heedless poets might suppose.

You need only look at her brow to know
that this lady of illusions is dressed in the colour of bone,
and carries a skull crowned with roses in her hands.

The others eat home-made bread, watered
with the characteristic tears of the epoch.

                    *

A green moon wearing a purple halo
Appears above the blue mist of the Sierra Nevada

At twilight we live in a half-erased dream
Everything slowly evaporates
We're left in a desert of rose and dead silver

Our flesh hurts from so many bright stars
In India the nights are not more aromatic

The face of the town turns pale
And in the streets that open toward the fields
There is the murmur of an abandoned harbour

In front of my door
A woman sang a lullaby
Like a ribbon of gold
Extending to the limits of the world

Ah little carnation
Of the most secret path . . .

I love the clear water and the turbid star.

The Banks of the Ohio

The buses would come sometimes three times a week, sometimes twice depending on the weather. They would leave Lubnava-Serbiny, the nearest town of any consequence, very early in the morning and make their way slowly along the valley of the interminable River Sorb, before heading up into the mountains. The passes were formidable, their road-sides punctuated with makeshift crucifixes commemorating the travellers who had succumbed to landslides, blizzards or unskilled drivers. The buses were battered, ingrained with dirt. We could hear their brakes screaming some miles away as they approached late in the evening.

It was not to be expected that persons of any distinction would alight at our village. Ours was one of the remotest corners of the Empire, – the butt of many jokes concerning ignorance and bad weather. The few tourists who sometimes found themselves marooned among us looked about with obvious amazement that they could have landed in a place so devoid of interest, without a castle or a mansion, with a church hardly distinguishable from a barn. Though surrounded by crags and forests we had never learnt to be picturesque. We were an obstinate, practical people whose festivals were few. But each year a man would arrive who seemed to justify the existence of the village, seemed to take it into the embrace of the great world beyond the mountains.

He would usually arrive at the beginning of autumn when the first violent winds came down from the passes to denude the trees. It was a time of regret, a time when longings rose up amidst us like mansions of clouds or leaves. And we, – I mean the young people of the village – would listen for the screaming of the brakes. No distant hunting horn ever sounded more melancholy or full of promise as the sound echoed and approached, echoed and retreated. Then the bus would swerve to a stop in a puddle. Then *he* would alight! I mean *The Traveller*. Then we would see the marvellous suitcase lowered from the steps of the bus, emblazoned with the labels of Nice and New York, Cairo, Stamboul, Buffalo, Bangkok, Paris and Manchester. We had little knowledge of these places and yet the vivid patchwork of the suitcase expressed them all to us. We walked along the broad avenues of these cities; we visited their museums, parks and restaurants; we encountered their most notable citizens and resided for weeks in their most expensive hotels. In truth, of course, very few of us had been further than Nysh, our dismal provincial capital, which history had largely neglected since an efficient Turkish massacre in the sixteenth century.

As soon as he alighted we would gather around him full of questions:

'Are the fogs of London as beautiful as they say?

Is it true that the Holymen of India can remove their eyes from their sockets and still see more clearly than you or I?

In Burma aren't there cities of pagodas infested with vultures?

Do the women of Russia dress entirely in furs and jewels rescued from the bellies of fish?

Isn't it true that in France in the Spring the young women dance on the bridges while the young men sing to them from boats moored beneath?

Don't persons in Egypt dwell in the tombs of their ancestors?

In China, I hear that the people are averse to all forms of direct statement.

In certain islands of the Indonesian archipelago a person is shunned if he or she is not at all times graceful.

In parts of Africa aren't ebony masks of family members buried beneath hearthstones?

In Japan it is the custom, is it not, for newly-weds to leap from waterfalls?

In America the automobiles are as large as yachts.

Are all Eskimos tattooed?'

Sometimes he would make some evasive, tantalizing reply, but more often he would merely shake his head and walk off in the direction of the inn. There he would stay for two months or three. He would rarely go out, or if he did so it was at a time when no one saw him. We never discovered why he came. It was thought that he came to relax, to escape from the wonders and anxieties of the great world, and perhaps to work at some personal project, – an account of his travels for example. He would not talk about his experiences which remained as mysterious to us as the life of the distant capital. He would not answer idle questions but if someone should approach him in need of advice or information concerning something vital to their existence his response was always sober and generous. There might sometimes be irony in his narrow smile, but never condescension. His learning amazed us but his manner was never boastful or arrogant and his advice was always found to be good. He was regarded with great respect, as a man of knowledge who had chosen to come among us, and yet after a time a certain resentment would begin to show itself, shadowing almost imperceptibly the unvarying courtesy with which he was treated. What was his purpose? What was his interest in our lives? He seemed to be observing us from a great distance. Gossips would remark that he drank more brandy than was wise and rose too late in the day. He would always leave before this resentment became open hostility. It was the crowning courtesy.

Many theories and suppositions surrounded him: he was a philosopher, a poet, a scientist, a disillusioned priest, the youngest son of an aristocratic family, or only a man who had failed in love. But a maid who, in a moment of forgetfulness, entered his room without knocking obstinately claimed he was a photographer. She found him, apparently hard at work, kneeling on the floor and so absorbed that he did not at first notice her. The table, the bed, the walls and most of the floor of the room were covered with photographs of cities, geographies and peoples that obviously could not exist, for the people had many eyes and were winged, and the buildings (which seemed to defy the laws of gravity) surpassed in size and grandeur the great monuments of the capital: there were buildings balanced on a point like inverted pyramids and pencil-thin towers enmeshed in winding ramps and elevated causeways. Her accounts were confused and contradictory. She had only glimpsed the pictures for a moment and many of them were indistinct, out-of-focus as if taken in great haste. She was a simple girl and many people doubted her word. True, there weren't many books in the village, but she might have seen books of fairy-stories or an illustrated Bible, since the winged people sounded very like cherubim or seraphim, yet she remained tearfully insistent that she had seen what she had seen, that the pictures were not drawings or paintings, that she had not 'made it up'. Furthermore there is no doubt that she had been greatly alarmed by what she saw. The Traveller, for his part, seems to have been more horrified and embarrassed than angry at her intrusion. He looked at her and she ran, – along the corridor and down the stairs until she came to rest on a bench before the inn where the proprietress comforted her.

Her reports were discussed for many years, – years in which he did not appear – and inevitably distortion and exaggeration did their work. What else could account for the floating city inhabited by giant cats, the forest of sprouting oblongs, the intelligent fire, or the Emperor in the glass garden? These were not images of our present time, however distant they might be in space. They were the images of his absence or of marvels the world did not contain.

Some five years later he returned, and we saw that he was old. The suitcase was horribly scarred, many of its labels obliterated, and there were no new ones that we could see. I remember my mother saying that now he had come to die. 'But why here,' I asked, 'where he is admired but knows nobody?' She could not answer but held to her opinion. It was the beginning of winter. The next day he appeared in hiking clothes and announced that he wished to visit an old monastery located two days journey south of the village, in the direction of Varna. He wanted to know whether its frescoes really were as fine as certain intrepid nineteenth-century travellers had reported. We assured him that the frescoes had been badly damaged by gunfire in the civil wars, and that the inclement winters of recent years would surely have obliterated what remained. We further warned him of the dangers of such an expedition at that time of year. But he was obstinate. His face closed and he shouldered his pack. There was no farewell committee, – such a thing would have embarrassed him – but as he left the village many people appeared at their doors and windows. As he passed out of sight snow began to fall. We did not see him turn round, but perhaps he looked back towards us from beyond that veil, and perhaps he thought of us with some affection. We did not see him again. After a month had passed the proprietress of the inn summoned the courage to open the suitcase but found that it contained nothing but an alarm-clock and a dictionary. And soon we forgot about him. The times were difficult. Buses came only once a week. Violent changes came from which our remoteness did not protect us, and soon we all had to travel, – not in order to discover the wonders of the world, but in order to escape destruction. This is what I will always regret, that my travelling was forced. What I had dreamed of so many times brought only terror and fatigue, and everywhere I felt I was in the same place: each place was an ignorant village with its priests, its mothers and its tyrants.

I have come to rest at last, – if 'rest' is the term – in a one-bedroom apartment, twenty stories up in a high-rise by the muddy Ohio River. As I write helicopters circle above the disorderly crowds swarming at the riverfront. They are protesting the recent killings. There can be no end to this though forty years have passed.

A Long Encounter

for Maggie Paley

Only the dead don't know
what heaven's like. For the rest
extrapolation is possible.

To meet someone for the first time
and immediately adore them, as if
they were the sun, would be one instance.

131

I don't mean you should fall in love
with this person, simply that when they speak
from the far side of a littered table

you should know you have entered a new country,
and its landscape, architecture and songs
will continue to embrace and fascinate you

through long years. An avenue has opened
and its trees are pricked with lights.
There is nothing you can't afford, if what

is expended is sympathy. These people
are to be treasured and celebrated
as if each were a public holiday, –

the planting of a first harvest
after a long and terrible voyage,
the construction of the first house in a wilderness.

The Golden Windows

for Paco

Who knows what drives us to persist
after a sleepless night, stencilled
with the vivid troubles of someone else's youth,

in the reading of a tedious saga
in which darkness prevails until the eleventh hour,

when the kitchen still waits
to be installed, the phone needs to be
connected, and the golden windows
glimmer dimly, at all times of the day,
on the far side of a filthy airshaft
six stories high? So today

a boy brought you a purple iris
and it lives in a bottle. How
did it get itself, how do I get myself
into this peculiar situation –
like suddenly waking on the streets
of a foreign city? No doubt –

'a wink and it is gone'
but the eye stays open like the mouth
of a tunnel leading under a river
and the avenues, tall as obelisks,
don't forsake you but fill you with their voices,
and the blue breath of autumn;

and all the windows of the street begin to shimmer
with the syllables of a message you cannot receive.

Move on. Take a hand. Accept this song.

The Monuments

Each year the monuments grew larger.
The citizens demanded this.
As their lives got worse they wanted
longer staircases to descend, towering fountains...

Taxes were increased. A famine settled in.
An inexplicable epidemic appeared.
Autumn was rain-sodden. So,
they collected funds for a new work

in the form of a giant, granite pineapple
encircled by a narrow staircase,
so difficult to climb some said
it symbolized life or friendship.

The monuments meant nothing of course.
The misfortune seemed undeserved.
At parties the food was served
on plates in the form of clouds

that descended from the ceiling,
and under each unseasonal strawberry
a gold leaf was set. Despite these strategies
the general melancholy increased.

Poems concerned themselves
with childhood, autumn and failure,
although it was understood that these took the place
of events too unbearable to discuss.

Work resumed on the pineapple.
It was decided to enclose it within a transparent
sphere inscribed with a poem concerning
autumn and failure. Meanwhile

in the downtown area, work began on a new
staircase, some 900 feet high, leading to
a colossal weeping eye. On rainy days
citizens would gather to watch the way

it vanished sweetly into mist,
but no one dared to place a foot
on even the lowest, shining step:
'This is art,' they said, 'We cannot use it.'

Funeral Preparations in the Provinces

One morning in autumn father died after a long, but not too painful ill-
ness. There was no time for expressions of grief. The whole family
thought of the work that lay ahead. It was unthinkable that father's
funeral should be improperly furnished. Mother was indefatigable,
attending to every detail. First they built the two horses and the chariot
out of wickerwork. Mother insisted that the horses had to look lively

and the chariot must be sturdy. She reasoned that since father had always enjoyed travelling whenever he had the opportunity, now that he had so much leisure time, he would doubtless want to travel the length and breadth of the next world, meeting its famous men, viewing its splendid landscapes. In the chariot they placed certain things he might need on his travels – a water-flask, a satchel with many compartments, a sunhat and a short cape to keep off the rains. A chariot was not the most convenient means of transport, of course, but mother reminded them that they were an old family, and they must think of the great days when their ancestors had been the esteemed advisors of emperors and statesmen.

Secondly, they built the house. It was really a small palace, all in miniature. They included all the furnishings he might need, from tables and chairs to mirrors and candlesticks. The kitchen was amply equipped with jars of herbs, spices and sauces, besides steamers, ladles and shining woks. In the dressing-room they hung his favourite dressing-gowns, his best suits and a tiny, grey fedora. In the study his flute rested on a sideboard, and in the same room was a black grand piano – something he had never possessed in life but had always desired. The library contained all the novels he had ever enjoyed, with pride of place given to *Madame Bovary* and *The Dream of the Red Chamber*. And because she worried that he might get bored during eternity (at least until she joined him) mother also included all the other novels she could think of – the longer the better – complete sets of Balzac, Dickens, Richardson, Stendhal, Tolstoy and Proust. The task of writing the names of authors and novels in gold on the spines of these miniature books (the actual pages of the books were mostly blank) fell to the eldest son. As may be imagined he suffered agonies in the task, and when it was completed his eyes were so red with strain that he looked as if he had been crying for days. And because the house had too many rooms for one man to keep clean and tidy – even if his youth should be returned to him in the after-life – mother also thought it wise to include servants, two charming girls and a handsome boy. She was determined that their faces should wear expressions of *absolute devotion*. This was very difficult to achieve in such small figures but the youngest son was very good at this kind of thing, and at last everything was completed to her satisfaction. Or so they thought.

By now they had worked for several days, almost without sleeping, but the charming appearance of father's model palace made it all seem worthwhile. It was at this point that mother announced that father had always loved gardening so they must, of course, make a garden for him. This came as something of a surprise to the children since they could only remember their father sitting or strolling in the garden, and that very infrequently. Most of the time he preferred to keep to his study from whence they would often hear the sound of his flute issuing, cool and a little melancholy, in the evenings. But it was impossible to argue with their mother who, besides, was a widow in mourning. They would have been social outcasts if it had become known that they had done so, and since the three daughters had done most of the gardening during father's lifetime – it was they who set about making a garden for him now.

They worked with passion and imagination and when they had finished everyone agreed that they had excelled themselves. There were winding, white-sanded paths (for which they used finely ground sugar), and willows made of wire painted green drooped over pools made of mirror-glass on which paper lotuses were firmly glued, and there were lanterns the colour of jade and pavilions from the eaves of which hung the smallest bells in the world (and these were made from scraps of kitchen foil). Also there were shrines and tinsel waterfalls and chrysan-themums the colour of burnished bronze. The three daughters fairly considered the delights of their garden to be inexhaustible. Even mother had difficulty concealing her pride in her clever daughters – why you'd almost think they were sons! And yet she was a little disappointed that there were no carp in the pools, and perhaps they should have pro-vided at least a brook and a boat since father had always enjoyed rowing on the river (which was so enormous they could not represent it), but she had to admit that there was no time left for these extensions and revisions. It was time to bury father.

It was a blustery, rainy day when they set out with the horses, the chariot, the house, the garden and father's stiff corpse loaded onto a cart and covered with an awning for protection. As they started out the rain set in with renewed force. Even the chrysanthemums wore a defeated air. (I mean the real chrysanthemums in the real, unkempt garden of the real, dilapidated house.) Dark clouds moved swiftly across the sky like torn rags. The old nag that was pulling the over-loaded cart seemed, on several occasions, inclined to give up. The cart-wheels stuck fast in mud time and again. When, at last, they reached their destination the whole family was soaked to the skin and exhausted, and mother's umbrella had blown inside out so often that a number of spokes were broken. Looking at the cemetery they almost despaired. How were they to light a pyre with the rain falling so heavily and the ground such an ocean of mud? But Fate smiled on them, for the rain ceased suddenly, the wind dropped, and the kindling, which had been stored beneath the corpse during the journey, was still relatively dry.

So they set father on the pile of kindling and around him they disposed the funeral furnishings in ceremonious fashion. After several failed attempts the fire took and, urged on by the autumn wind, soon grew to a small inferno. Mother reached into her fat leather purse and scattered a handful of banknotes into the flames. Now he would want for nothing. They watched for a long time while their days of passionate endeavour rose to the heavens in a dark cloud. They could not think what to say, and at last they wept. They wept for their father who was dead, but they wept much more for the prancing horses, the elegant chariot, the gleaming kitchen, the devoted servants, the piano, the flute, the library of noble books and the garden of a thousand delights.

It came to them at last that something had gone out of the world and would never return to them however much love, imagination and skill they might expend. They saw the end of everything in the black cloud above them, and also they saw the wisdom of their ancestral customs. Only mother remained dry-eyed. When the fire was out and the ashes were interred she fetched a deep sigh and, for a moment, grief descended on the worn features of her face. There was a long silence. At last she shrugged and said: 'Well, I don't know if it works, but at least he can't complain. Everything has been done correctly.' She further reflected that after so much expense there was no money left for a gravestone – not even the simplest gravestone with the mere name of the dead person written on it. All that would be left was a low mound, and this, she reminded them, had been the fate of many an emperor, so they should not feel embarrassed.

Pianola Music (Double Portrait)

1

I bought a bird-house
but, for a month, no birds seemed to call.
Now they come, but they're only sparrows or grackles...
On certain mornings it's hard not to interpret
like the gloomiest scholar. The sparrows
are students, perhaps, without a thought in their heads
except the ones their adored teacher planted there.
And the grackles? Well, the grackles
with their voices like the sound of crude,

wind-up toys, must be critics of course: they dump
on anything stationary in the parking-lot.

Nothing can be relied upon it seems.
Not the bird-house. Not the house.
Or the love people bear for you,
though they bear it obviously like a floral basket.
It is something you'd like to accept, but where
would you put it? Could it live
as a punctuation at the turn of the stairs
or on the long table in the sun-flooded kitchen?

The light is a base you touch each day,
yet it reflects off any willing surface,
it deflects and diffuses the dark thoughts of separation
night intruded like a claw. Even
your own outline dissolves in this solution,
and the gilded spines of old adventure novels catch fire
with a fire like that of some rural catastrophe
that actually harms no one, –

the crops are all safe and shadows cast by
skyscrapers of flame are made of some gorgeous
purple stuff that unravels over the landscape,
collecting in spoiled heaps at the horizon.

The spectators in the fields like it so much
they join hands and drink to the event.

2

The ordinary blessings are
entered in the journal.

There are windows and doors that open.
There is a veranda for the summer.
There is conversation in the evenings
and the preparation of meals.
There are patriotic tunes,
Episcopalian hymns...
(They'll let you sing anything.)

138

The street leading down to the river
on which only garages seem to open,
painted hard-to-describe, faded shades of grey and plum
seems a permanent, cool backwater of autumn
where the 'Tree of Heaven' drops its leaves.

The courthouse square is beautiful today, –
it is so much how you always wanted it to be,
classically so, shaded by trees, bordered by churches, –
not impervious, but crisp and resistant
to the mill-race of too much randomness.
That's why you petitioned against the new bandstand:
it was already *enough* in the words of the chorale.

So, you have looked at the square,
you have looked at the mountains and the river
(and you have looked at the paintings of these scenes)
you have looked at the woods in autumn
and the houses in the form of Greek temples.

If you still don't know quite what to make of it all,
who would, given so much material for vision
and these things are like you a little, aren't they,
as a favourite coat becomes like you, and becomes you?

from **The Burnt Pages**

In Rainy Country

It was already the landscape of the past,
streaked with illusionary colours –
all of it displaced, tilted at a crazy angle,
blazing with the rare sunlight of a rainy country,
all of it impossible though it was only the place
where you had lived for too many years –

all of it *below, behind,*
the tamed river curling out of the burnt blue hills
crossed by the massive red arches of a viaduct
(and none of it to be seen again, except through fog),
the city bristling and blurring as it sank away,
knowing it had failed like Ephesus,
a port the great ships no longer visited, a place to leave.

The world was an aureole
surrounding a small, sealed window,
and you turned from the glass astonished and in tears
at the start of a new trajectory.

The air was so sweet
on your arrival it was as if
the trees in the park blossomed, although the year was ending,
ending in glory. You had crossed the ocean. Now
you stepped from the avenue into the rotunda
and smiled toward the statue of a woman. Wine was poured
at the top of the curving stairs and the mirrors
were filled with the faces of those who justified
all your waiting, messengers from another life.
Each one arrived with a nimbus, each smile sang
of an understanding that would last beyond
the framing curtains of this night.

There would be multiplications and extensions,
polyphonic variations on the deathless theme, which now
you held in your hand like a brilliant maple leaf
salvaged from the ruin of a noble valley.

So if the cold abraded your ears,
or if your coattails blew about in the merciless
wind of Seventh Avenue, it did not matter;
you were on your way to purchase music or help love prosper.

What is left behind is irretrievable,
but continues like a melody
whose logical and grieving progression nothing can halt.

Impossible not to think of it now –
the horror that fell on my father like a wolf and nearly tore him out of
    life.
And Mother? Mother suffers more quietly,
a weeping scale on a piano, and the piano distant.

Forgetting

I lived in suburbs so long,
I may never get over it. Yet those days
are obscure as the details of a drunken stupor,
in which, perhaps, you denounced enemies
or declared your love, while mist and the enamel
of moonlight settled in the empty canal.

Where were the grocery stores
when you needed them at three in the morning?
Where was the sense of immediate association
with people who just happened to be
in great numbers on the same street as you?

The world's largest and most vulgar cathedral
rises on your right; on your left the forecourt
of a mausoleum is overgrown with grass.

Who's dead in there?
you wonder, and why is it always
impossible to take home all the flowers
you saw in the florist's: not just the purple tulips,
the yellow tulips, and lilies spotted with blood,
but all the flowers whose names
you never had the patience to learn?

I know I mix the present with the past,
but that's how I like it:
there is no other way to go on.

The bungalows drift off indifferently
and sink in the reservoir. Only
the carefully tended rose beds remain
floating on the surface. The uneven steps descend
through young willows and sprouting weeds
to absolute mud and rushes –
origin of this ignominious kingdom –
and the unprofitable sunsets are shut down.

Once, under that signature of light,
we lived in the dream of a past that never existed
except in the ogival arches
and Ionic capitals of doorways painted white.
Now a strong leader has come amongst us,
and, in consequence, we know nothing.

The future is a locked factory gate.
Leaves cling in thousands to the chain-link fences,
but the trees that once stood, bigger than clouds,
overshadowing all the houses I lived in
are cut down. I remember
glowing, unlit candles, and some kind
of polished wooden jewels kids in cemeteries
collected in conditions close to ecstasy
(they vanished long ago, folded
into a thick cloak of years).

The sky above the roof was crazy with swallows.
We looked out of slits smaller than our eyes
to see the lilac die or the pear tree break into flames.

Prelude to Mammon

When the autumn came they ran
to the opera to applaud the horses.

Star-systems suspended
from their drooping shoulders, they complained
that the slaves were the wrong colour.
The children were grave, the horses black and plumed.

The sky was like the lining of a dome
in Ravenna, the sunlight an arrow.

On solitary evenings when
the pavements glistened
they snarled and paced in the shadow
of dark armoires, or giant buildings
resembling them. Students of metamorphosis,

they knew the question was not
when the new book or film or concerto
would be finished, but when it could be
abandoned. They loved the empty spaces

like perfect fields of purple loosestrife
in which planets might appear
in the torn shifts of extinct mythologies,
and perhaps favour them with a word or phrase:
'Not now. Not yet. Perfidious.
Mask of bone that once gave song.'

Three Scenes

1

Indigence like a fog infects
the folkloric woodlands and trailers.
An axe is heard. Insects
descend at evening toward
the magnet of her very pale arm
from which the woollen shawl
has slipped. The atmosphere is
good/ not good for the child.
Sometimes a violin or bird
screeches its two wrong notes nightlong.

The empty cashbox sinks in the clear river.
How far away is the city? No matter
how far, it is time to be going.

The city is distant by many waterways and islands.
Its towers rise beside a bay.
Each ferry has a different
name and colour. Let us travel
on the blue *Berenice*,
the white *Irene*, the lonely *Anna*.
The child will laugh at the waves/
the child will scream and hide itself
in the Greek folds of the shawl.
There will be a sound like an axe falling.

2

The woman's hair is like a lion's mane.
In the café, in a whisper, she tells the child
the story of the travelling salesman's ghost.

Rain falls slant against the elevated train.
At noon the light remains dim. The tear in
the window blind is big enough for one blue eye.

Between flower beds in the shape of sunbursts
the local militia stand at attention. The statues
seem to say, 'There's always a war somewhere.'

The summer is vanishing back into cement.
A sanitation truck passes, plastered with leaves.
In the square the yellow tents are folded.

The murderer complains that his mother never loved him,
and continues: 'You have to go to the edge,
and when you get there you can't go no further.' Yes,

and the trick is to walk elegantly, without shuddering
above the girders, and garbage and distant fires.
Word is, 'down there they drown you in your car.'

3

Caught up in the concerns of the day
(a mild Wednesday in October) he resolved
to stay where he was and think about these matters.
It had been a year of disturbances, storms out of season.

Or he decided to set out at once for the mountains
and the snows, a place beneath a blue pine...
Surely a life of the instincts was preferable to
the rehearsal of Hellenistic philosophies?

Sitting on the warm stones of the harbour,
he reflected: 'All decisions are hazardous,
including the decision not to decide. To know
the names of all the boats and to have consulted

the long-range forecasts is not enough, nor
to be enchanted by maps showing the ragged
outlines of glaciers and fjords, nor to think
of star-like flowers under the hooves of elk,

when your heart cannot ignore the new towers
of the city, clad in red marble and black glass.
Is it possible to abandon these atriums,
these concert halls, cafés and record stores?

Regarded coldly, the choices look meagre:
a) moving on, b) staying put, c) personal extinction,
and d) turning back, which is equivalent to c)...'
On the esplanade contented couples strolled

toward a lurid conflagration in the west,
unperplexed by dull-witted abstractions
that grazed above their heads. A woman
turned to him and asked: 'What keeps us here,

where the very air seems a menace? There is
no war, yet the streets are littered with the dying,
and to take a walk is to step on outstretched hands.'
He replied: 'There are reasons for disquiet.

There are rumours of a plot against the Boss,
and a new outbreak of Platonism has alarmed
the clerics, yet your desire for a haven seems
a possible regression, a romance of sturdy hill forts

after plague has emptied the cities; but this is not
such an age, not yet. We are alive here and living.
Let us go home while it is still light. Let us
behave in the manner of travellers returning.'

The Strategikon, or Don't Go Out of the Door

Since he came from an old and noble family,
we may assume that General Cecaumenus
wanted for nothing. There were wines in his cellars,
sweetmeats at his table; on the walls of his chambers
Samson and Achilles, David and Alexander
performed their heroic exploits in stucco and paint,
and beyond the doors of his mansion the manifold
delights of the greatest city of that time
were spread out as if for a banquet: the wharves

146

were crowded with ships; under the colonnades
the shops were stocked with finely crafted
enamels, ivories and silks;
solemn music sounded from the churches,
and the portals of the Sacred Palace, and through
the crowds of Latins, Persians, Jews and Greeks
the great ladies, in the afternoon, hurried home,
accompanied by slaves and clouds of rare perfume,
for an evening of recitations from the Classics
or the latest erotic novels. Yet these are the words
that General Cecaumenus, in his wisdom, saw fit
to set down in his famous *Strategikon*:
'Never let a friend reside for long in your home,
for he may seduce your wife. Rather let him
lodge elsewhere, and send him the necessary food.
Secure your daughters as if they were criminals.
Avoid all parties. In sum, unless you are about
the emperor's business stay at home with your most
trusted servants, and hoard supplies against emergencies.
Only in this way can a wise man hope to avoid evil.'

New and Selected Poems

To the confusion of the casual visitor, the city of S— contains an old
cathedral like a fortress, a new cathedral like a theatre, and a prison like
a cathedral. This will give you some idea of the elevated wisdom of its
inhabitants.

*

He says he will catch the two o'clock train from New York to
    Philadelphia –
The fool! Philadelphia is a town in western Asia Minor.
Manuel Palaeologus sat on a white horse before its walls and wept.

*

147

Portuguese night, Aegean night, Manhattan night, Pacific night –
O night like a tattered curtain reluctant to descend!
Moon! Lovely as a Korean grocery store at midnight...

*

There were once poets everywhere hereabouts. Impossible to compute the number of street signs and baroque plaques commemorating them. A whole family of them lived for generations in the drowned convent of Santa Clara, but, alas, they have all moved away, perhaps as a result of the frequent disputes over matters of style that so often degenerated into devastating street brawls. Things got so bad that the cafés became uninhabitable, but the discriminating tourist may still admire the ruins of the Tower of the Poets, the Fountain of the Poets, the Palace of the Poets, the Racecourse of the Poets and the Abattoir of the Poets. Indeed, on occasion, a slim volume can still be found poking out of a mound of rubble. But, of course, if you find one you must at once report it to the ministry.

*

The child who still hadn't learnt that the statues could not respond stood by the green pool (in which a family of goldfish were quarrelling over a crust of bread) shouting Athena! Adonis! Actaeon! while his mother called his name impatiently from the gate.

*

His lovely red-haired wife having died giving birth to them, a man discovered that his twin children – a girl and a boy – were geniuses. Without any teaching they composed music and poetry, and early on showed an interest in philosophy and the natural sciences. Their paintings took the form of mysterious allegories concerning which connoisseurs spilt futile rivers of ink.

Their father loved them absolutely, yet feared that they might not respect him, but they were so truly intelligent that they understood that their father – though less gifted than they and sometimes a little foolish – was nevertheless a good man. He, for his part, perceived in all their works the many colours of their mother's hair and skin, the gleam her green eyes had on certain evenings.

*

In this country of orange groves, orange roofs and rice paddies
It took me some time to understand the ways of the maids.
In the first week they will mislay your laundry wilfully,
Replacing it with that of some wealthy financier or property developer,
And of course you cannot go out in these preposterous garments –
It would be better to go naked. In the second week
They will perhaps deliver the beautifully laundered robes and headgear
Of a Tibetan lama, and this is an improvement –
One can at least go out to a café dressed in this fashion.
In the third week a subtle understanding is reached,
And a handsome necktie appears amid the sleek folds of evening gowns.

*

The grandmother in her black dress
Gathers her beautiful granddaughter to her breast
(Where a sickle moon hangs from a long chain)
And says: 'My darling, you must not sleep
With attractive young men, for they will write you sonnets,
They will write you whole sequences of despairing lyrics in *vers libre*.
So you see it would be terribly cruel of you to share their beds.'
And the granddaughter glances toward
The volume of despairing sonnets
Burning in her raincoat pocket.

*

    I was sitting on my balcony one evening trying to trace the source of a particularly strong odour of honeysuckle when suddenly a bugle began to blow, and an enormous image of Hercules appeared in the sky. What a hero! He leaned so close I could feel his breath, which was hot and smelled of oregano, but I did not like the gleam in his eye, and ran quickly into the house, slamming the shutters behind me.

    I picked up a book I had been reading. Everything was calm again. Freya Stark was still sailing along the coast of Lycia. I ignored the loud thumping on the shutters.

Weekends in West Connecticut

It is a place of enormous trees
and a million stridulant insects.
At the centre of so much counterpoint
sleep is impossible, and the garden is crushed
into something like a pill the night will swallow.

Of course the light still loiters in the streets,
and the houses with their varied porches are charming
as musical boxes filled with *Rückert* lieder,
but what is it causes this putative mayor of Westport
and his wife to decorate their master bedroom
with crude agricultural implements?
It looks like a torture chamber... Outside,

blue spruces, red oaks, white pines all loom,
and the undergrowth's lush and tangled as Mandarin prose.
You imagine boundless forests, but the path is barred
a short way in at the outer precincts of another shrine
to domesticity, glowing through mutinous leaves,
and the sun, forgotten token, drops somewhere out of sight.

Nothing is held in common here:
corporations build their headquarters beside
absurd, idyllic millponds, and the city towers,
the open lands are driven away,
ever further over the unglimpseable horizon.
Confused by so much opulence and uniformity
it would be easy to forget the way out,
easy to forget that such a thing was needed.

A land without horizon or sunset is a safe place –
safe as the bedroom of your childhood
with its yellow walls and deceiving pictures
of friendly grownups and loquacious animals,
but when the last bricks of these walls have crumbled,
when the last shreds of those images have been blown
into the ocean, you are left alone in the muggy garden
with the irritable cat, amid a swarm of cries.

You hold in your hand a guide to
Swedish folk art in America.

Several Romantic Novels

Before the body that almost destroyed them, masters of eloquence gape
  merely.
There are no words for this, or too many words that never quite fit –
each a Cinderella's shoe to these blunt objects of sense. *Exempla*:
The door opened with a sigh. You had forgotten you had left it
  unlocked –
and at the dark end, like a funnel, of such a cold day! This is something
  to be watched,
yet negligence can allow sudden reversals into summer heat even as
  winter advances:
a cardinal attempts, with its one steel note, to stitch the garden back
  together,
fastening a geranium to a shirt of snow. But the bird stays hidden.
Does it matter who entered? His arrival is, anyway, a gust, pushing you
  back
into a chamber of distorted perspective, of distorting mirrors, and the one
who has arrived follows, becomes concentrated like a pillar while *your*
  body disperses –
a hand like a torn flag, an eye big as a geographer's globe, your neck
a leaning tower about to fall into as many pieces as there are leaves on
  the unswept lawn.
How long can this shuddering continue? The autumn slows. The hours
  cannot withstand it.
It travels under the skin of highways whose trees seem studded with
  garnets, with blood-droplets;
even the truck stops are quaking, and the prairie of the dog convulses
  into ravines
vaulted by fire, floored with glass, until you arrive at the summit of a
  rock formation
resembling a steamboat, but some miles from any river.

Below (below deck)

a thousand fabulous dinner parties are in progress and, unaware
of what is happening to the landscape, your host proffers, in greeting,
  his wooden hand.
He is a stranger to you, as are all his guests so happily absorbed in
the convivial mood-music and margaritas when, to you, it seems time
to talk of *the irrational*, time to make an opera out of the earthquake,
even as the prongs penetrate the breasts of the enormous dead bird,
and some damned Vivaldi concerto stutters into life like a knitting
  machine.

The urge to shout 'Fire!' or at least, 'Look, *I'm* on fire!' becomes
    irresistible,
yet, in truth, these are the kindest and most charming of people – so
much so that I think all their children must be chamber-musicians –
and this is the kindest and most charming of towns, a town of porch
    swings and pumpkin-lanterns
wherein the most deviant perspectives, the most grotesque peccadilloes
    are
tethered securely to the gold cupola of the capitol. There is nothing to
    fear,
the citizens are on watch and will surely return the scattered parts of
    your body
should they find them: 'I recognize this, sir, as your penis. You left it
on a bench in the mall, close by a cut-price shoe outlet, I believe.' So
perhaps it is OK to leave your door ajar again if that is your mood,
only remember there are some violent natural phenomena that
take the form of men or women. (*He* was a cyclone at least; he has
    returned
to a remote state with a name like that of sexual lubricant.) Other
instances might be offered of which the scream of a damaged car heater
would be one, but for now what you had forgotten covers the occasion
    like a mantle –
evening assuming a profounder blue, the dead awaking in a glance,
and it is time to be attentive, watching for the apparition of a red bird,
for the green bowl of the garden to fill with snow. There remains
the no one who came and the no one who departed, his growing legend.

The Middle Kingdom

In those days we spent our time
sitting quietly in softly lighted rooms
designed for that purpose, trying not
to let any involuntary line of thought
arrive at its logical (and, of course,
regrettable) conclusion: namely,
that our days were numbered.

We were all well-fed and warmly clothed,
and experienced no misgivings on this account.
The oceans were calm and shallow,
the rivers stocked with salmon. Each spring
brilliantly coloured birds passed over
on their way to northern lakes and hills.
Poems were often penned concerning
their brief and glorious transit. When
they returned in autumn we succumbed
to appropriate feelings of mild regret.

Our figurative art gave no hint of the fact
that male animals experienced erections,
nor were children obliged to light the match
that would incinerate their families.
Similarly it was not considered necessary
to rip your opponent's lips from his face,
or force him to digest his ears.

How slow that time now seems,
how sweet, how gradual every graceful gesture!
But it is impossible to regret its passing
It was not a time of truth and realism.
The passage of migratory birds
did not accord to the facts, nor
the coming of spring, nor the love of mothers
for their children, nor a man's respect
for women, nor courtesy, friendship, honour...

Regret is impossible
(and, besides, nostalgia
is an imprisonable offence) now
that every issue is clear as blood,
bright as tears, and we live
in understanding even as we die.

My Egypt

The street is a horn the wind blows through –
a ram's horn, a car's horn, a French horn,
but its melody, though plangent, may not be
the one you want to hear right now.

The river tows its dreams,
consigned to the dim edge of existence,
reciting dull epics to desolate piers.
Many, you included, are still abed,
but already the avenues are crowded
with people like flags of more nations
than exist in the world. It is all
a pageant of some kind, though anxious
and colder than of late.

The last tropical rainstorms visit us.
It is a day in September full of whispers of anticipation.
It is a time of greetings like farewells and farewells like greetings.
For a depressing moment things seem foreordained,
entered in the prophetic ledger like age and decrepitude –
the thought of white hair and rising snowbanks,
burdened trees breaking with a crack.

Book of summer we have read you,
every word, and memorized the lines we need.
The colours turn. A single tree is purple, green and red,
and we begin to wonder if something really spectacular
will happen, like the installation on an endless
Von Sternberg staircase of the emperor or empress
of these events. We also wonder *how* it can happen
in times when the remarkable is expected, as the sun is expected
to rise, and even this seems to happen in memory –

memory which is endlessly revised
to suit the present image, to which the past
leads us by means of a strict gothic perspective.
How to account therefrom for your continual dreams
of the future which thrill and frighten you
like bombs dropping on the city of your birth?
A department store where, perhaps, your first pyjamas

were purchased goes up in flames, and the surviving streets
are black with a kind of joyful malice that is soon erased.

What are these flurries? Of snow? These heaps
of stuff, soiled or destined to melt? Mush of potsherds?
Glass of a mosaic? They are discarded in time like shoes or old books.
The seasons are like a day stretched over a year,
impossible to grasp, but we will be changed
at the turning of the year, changed for the better.

Scenes from Schumann

As in an old memoir, the rhododendrons were over.
Hunger persisted, and the light was weak –
the light of music and books, the light paintings cast
on bowls of fruit and tablecloths, to make them ours...

So the black dish was upturned,
and a fragment of it rolled with the peaches into
burnt grass nearby. It had been a long summer, and now
a glass vase in the shape of a hand stood up against

the perspective of hills and rain, dogs and daylilies.
We had known about the storm, perhaps for a century
before it happened, so much had been gathered in, protected
under awnings and arcades, yet the paintings were streaked,

and the scores curled into oblivion. It was impossible
to imagine the birth of the orchestra, as we once knew it:
it was a friend who had become many strangers, each
with a hat or facial feature, a scream or sigh

like the opening of a door that must remain shut.
We were all looking out from the windows of the library
toward the river that is not a river. The narrow lawn
looked very green after the rains, and the white chairs

were night animals caught in searchlights.
The urns showed well against the blue of the river,
and beyond them, the ruins of the old insane asylum,
covered in leaves, in the bronze colour of their bricks –

fading, as the lights came on in loops along the bridge,
festive as the illuminations of childhood. But
the vignettes were out of focus, the anecdotes faltered; the words
took off like birds from our lips, to circle an absence

that couldn't be named without turning the feast to ashes.
Not that the talk died. No, it grew brighter, like lights reflected
in swift, dark water. Only, at intervals, we seemed to hear
the river recalling the desolate passage of a bridal barge.

Smoke

It was late in the year
and forests were burning a long way off,
the day the smoke arrived, almost unperceived.
It came as a ghost, as many ghosts,
visible in the mouths of tunnels.

Now that your neighbour is dead,
you recall casual greetings on the stairs,
snatches of show tunes in corridors,
and you look down into that well –

that well of uncertain light and air – and see an absence
which neither snow nor corrosive rain efface,
and the absence returns your glance, it follows like a cur
extending its tongue of smoke toward your hand.

The smoke enters the lamplight and the bed.
The eyes are clouded, the eyes are abolished,
and the ears that drank in the old arias of desire.
Venice is diminished, and Rome,

their bells dulled, their restaurants emptied;
in Manhattan the towers shrink from the sky;
all places and all scenes become the less observed,
the less heard, the less loved.

In a city of burnt throats there can never be
enough sweet water to start the songs
and if you would dance, you must dance to the memory
of that lighted window the dusk carried off,

those hands preparing the evening meal,
skeletal hands fumbling among
the bottles of useless prophylactics,
those limbs and mouths, smoke we daily breathe.

But don't vanish, don't take the path to the river.
It is cold there and lonely,
and the sky is a burnt page. Stay –

you and you others. If we are not to become
a dispersed people of smoke,
the monument that is us must be built soon.

Following a Man

I was following a man
with a handsome, intelligent face
(the cheekbones high, the nose straight, the lips
sufficiently full), and judging by the shape
of his neck (an unfailingly reliable
indicator in my experience) a lithe, athletic
figure; or, to be more exact, he and I were merely walking
in the same direction along Seventh Avenue,
having earlier stood side by side in the Old Chelsea Post Office:
the day was Friday, June 9th, the time late afternoon,
and after only two or three blocks,
each full of its particular events and distractions
(such as dogs, clouds, paupers, hydrants, hairdressers),

I began to feel that I was almost in love with this man,
that, like a song, I would follow him anywhere...

Something about the way he slicked back his hair
delighted me, and I admired his beautiful raincoat
which so enhanced the easy masculine grace
of his movements. I was concentrating hard,
trying to take in all these details without giving
any cause for embarrassment (either on my part
or his) when he swerved into a newspaper store
between 16th Street and 15th, and I could think of no
plausible excuse for following him into that meagre space
where, surely, our eyes would have been forced to meet,
and I would have blushed (he being protected by a light tan).

In all likelihood he is lost to me, as
he would have been had that door been
the door to an elevator in an apartment building
bigger than all the pyramids combined.
Even if he should prove to be my near-neighbour
I doubt that I will ever see him again,
since in New York there are always too many
neighbours to keep track of (you hear
their footsteps, their voices and their music,
but it is difficult to attach these attributes
to a particular person, in much the same way
that an archaeologist may uncover the fragments
of a mirror but will never know the face
that, day by day, was reflected there)
but it is not as if he were dead. He exists
and will continue to do so for some time, perhaps
for many years, and as I walked without hesitation
directly past the store he had entered I was overcome
with a sudden feeling of elation at the thought
that it was within my power to record this incident
which is unexceptional
as the budding of pear trees in their season,
unrepeatable as the first sight of a great city.

Cigarettes

Problems of translation are, perhaps, not so great
between languages as between different versions
of the same language. Why, for example, does
'fag' mean homosexual in America, when,
in England, it means cigarette? Does this imply
that those who first observed the phenomenon
of smoking in the New World were homosexual?
This would cause some consternation on Columbus Day,
and, in all likelihood, the assumption is unjustified,
since Columbus and his crew were not English-speakers.
Yet, if we dismiss the idea of happy crowds of
homosexual Spanish or Italian mariners
returning to Europe with cigarettes in hand,
eager to introduce this new pleasure to their lovers,
we should perhaps concede that there is some connection
between the two ideas. It was Oscar Wilde, after all,
who described smoking as 'the perfect pleasure, because' –
he opined – 'it always leaves one unsatisfied.'
It is clear from this that he was thinking of sexual pleasure,
of the working-class youths with whom he so recklessly dined
in fashionable restaurants of the eighteen-nineties.
A cigarette is like a passion in that it is inhaled deeply
and seems to fill all the empty spaces of the body,
until, of course, it burns down, and is put out amid
the shells of pistachio nuts, or whatever trash
may be at hand, and the passion may leave traces
that in time will grow malignant: he who has taken pleasure
may die many years after in the room of an anonymous
hotel or hospital, under the blank gaze of a washstand,
a bad painting or an empty vase, having forgotten entirely
the moment that announced the commencement
of his dying. And perhaps he will not understand:
it is another false translation, like someone stumbling over
the word for cigarette in a new and intolerable language.

Revising the Atlas

It was just something I knew and thought I'd tell you.
Its relevance might be questionable, but that is no reason
not to draw attention to it, as one might to a carnation
crushed into the tarmac by a truck. I think I got the facts right
about 'the egg crown', the invasions, and the arrow that killed
the rebellious second cousin of the incestuous emperor
(who fired it, in what poison its barb was steeped),
but what are you to make of this information? I could say:
*That year the suburban palaces had to be rebuilt, for the sixth time
in a decade*, and that might produce the required sense of awe
and strangeness, also of revulsion at acts of inhumanity and wanton
destructiveness which, however, show no sign of stopping –
mosaic faces torn from the walls and the domes,
the little towns with no names burning all over the rumpled map.

Or I could continue: *At that time Western Europe
possessed no cities worthy of the name.* And you might reflect
that now we have too many of them, and they threaten to link up
like one horrible amorphous organism on a scale
so preposterous that everything begins to seem small, squalid,
    undistinguished –
Arches of Triumph, festal towers, canals, and churches all lost
in the general urban scrimmage. Or you might say: 'But that
is ancient history, the deadest of letters. Life today is so exciting
since we are daily menaced by the prospect of extinction
in a variety of novel forms, of which ecological ones are currently the
    most popular.'
So you return to your novel, written in sentences calculated
not to distress the syntax-impaired, about the adventures
of a ruthlessly ambitious yet somehow wonderful young woman,
beginning in the boondocks and ending at the headquarters
of the world's classiest perfume conglomerate, and taking in
poverty, riches, sex, irony struggle, and play, not to mention
an exhaustive kaleidoscope of despoiled but still lovely
North American landscapes along the way. And so to bed!

Yet, despite everything, isn't it good to be here
especially if, in summer, you can afford to spend your time
by some gleaming arm of the ocean with a steady supply
of cocktails at hand? Also music and X-rated videos.

Come the fall, the party circuit gets competitive, and even
the indigent can benefit, providing they have a couple of pairs
of decent shirts and pants. But I am still determined
to bend your ears, to turn your gaze back through leaf-fall
and cool breezes that bring news of the Azores or the Aleutians,
so that, reluctantly but with decision, I resort to
parallelism and human interest, the unhistorical factors:
Men shaved their beards and began to affect turbans.
Baggy pants became fashionable. Upper-class women appeared
more frequently in public, and took to giving literary soirées
in their uptown mansions. There was a craze for Islamic art,
and the erotic novel was revived for the first time in nearly a millennium.

But you turn up the TV reports of the latest
race- or drug-related murders, switching channels in the hope
that an accumulation of dull trivia will approximate to insight
(as if, with enough pebbles, you could build a Matterhorn),
or you are out the door on your way to a movie set in a colossal, painted
    city
that looks strangely like home, except that the colours are brighter,
    cleaner,
and the mechanism of the drawbridge is more immaculately
    Constructivist.
And you needn't worry, the hero's beautiful coat resists gunfire,
the sunset is glamorous as a billionaire's descent into bankruptcy,
a lavishly illumined liner, of archaic design, passes on the dark river,
and on its deck a swing band is playing close to the swimming pool
on which many happy couples are dancing. Ah! this is history
as we like to know it, administered by nostalgia's prefecture,
by means of which we escape the sensation that an earthquake has
    swept
all the sites of childhood away, and there is no harbour we can call our
    own!

Melancholy and fatigue
must follow any examination of the facts,
insofar as there are any that elude
the pervading glimmer of ambiguity,
our hope and curse. Today, for example, the radio warns
that the elderly and those with respiratory problems should stay
indoors, and no strenuous activity should be undertaken
lest there be faintings, seizures, infarctions, collapses –

a veritable Dance of Death on sidewalks, in gasping parks.
This announcement comes between Stravinsky's *Capriccio*
and a Schubert piano trio, and the brain divides
like a tenement full of contentious apartment dwellers. On cue,
I can't breathe. My head aches, my heart also, but I continue
to mutter as if quiet children were present who would hear me:
There were great disparities. Despite centuries of complaints
the colonnaded thoroughfare of the city was interrupted by
a quagmire into which pack animals often sank without trace.
The economic future of the state had been mortgaged to foreigners
who behaved with great arrogance, and were periodically massacred.
The plague arrived in a beautiful cloth from the East. Death
of one kind or another stared everyone in the face, but few
had the courage to return the gaze or take action. The angel
did not descend by the burnt pillar. And does not, still does not.

The Seventeenth Sermon

In the turbulent career of the patriarch Photios
there can have been few days more glorious
than Saturday, March 29th 867.
It was on this day that he delivered his seventeenth sermon,
'On the Inauguration of the Image of the Virgin',
in the great church of the Holy Wisdom,
in the presence of the emperors Michael III and Basil I.
It was Easter, and the long night of iconoclasm –
the rule of those 'shameful emperors now universally deplored' –
had ended. The patriarch indicated
a group of worshippers dressed all in white, men
who had recently abjured the execrable doctrines
of the Quartodecimans, according to whom Easter
should be celebrated on the fourteenth day of the lunar month,
whether or not is was a Sunday. As Photios
continued to speak with his customary eloquence and erudition,
the devout gathering could see in the apse behind him
the new image of the enthroned Virgin and her Child,
seeming to float on a gold ground, and flanked by the archangels
Michael and Gabriel. To Photios it seemed

as if the Virgin were about to speak, to explain
to any sceptics her paradoxical status as virgin and mother,
for her lips seemed of real flesh, pressed together and still
as in the sacraments. Her gaze was compassionate
yet detached, directed toward a child and eternity;
her image was a silent script from which both the learned
and the ignorant could acquaint themselves with the truths
of Christian doctrine. But a man
of Photios's intellectual refinement could not
countenance a merely didactic philosophy of art.
He did not neglect the aesthetic properties:
by its beauty and harmony of proportion
the image gave delight and strength to the spectator,
and predisposed the mind to accept the order of the universe.
All of this Photios further claimed was an act of restoration:
the church, though still scarred and wounded,
had now regained some of her ancient beauty; sadness was cast off,
and she was once again clothed in her bridal garment.
In this respect the patriarch was almost certainly mistaken,
since all the evidence suggests that the original decoration
of the church consisted of abstract vines and garlands
framing many simple representations of the cross.
Photios's 'forms imprinted on the tablet of the soul' did not
exist in the time of Justinian and Anthemius.

In the course of his sermon the patriarch also took care
to praise Michael and Basil, calling them
'a beloved pair of pious emperors, father and son,
shining in royal purple', but according to the histories
Michael was a notorious drunkard
given to loutish acts of vandalism, while Basil,
his adopted son, was an illiterate peasant,
born of a Slav mother and an Armenian father.
His magnificent physique had caught the emperor's eye
as he was passing by the palace stables one day,
and it seems likely that the two men became lovers.
It is certain that they shared the favours
of the same woman, one Eudocia Ingerina,
and as he delivered his sermon Photios must have thought
of the fate of his benefactor, the Caesar Bardas.
It has been said in Michael's defence that although
unfit to rule he allowed better men to govern for him,

chief among them his uncle the Caesar, enlightened
founder of the new university of the Magnaura Palace,
but in the spring of the previous year Basil
had killed Bardas in the presence of the emperor,
and immediately afterward was himself raised to the throne.
In the months that followed the seventeenth sermon
the two men grew suspicious of each other.
Michael drank while Basil made plans, disposing
of Michael on the evening of September 23rd 867.
Such were the two men Photios lauded as 'beloved' and 'pious',
and such was the beginning of the Macedonian golden age,
for against all expectation Basil ruled wisely,
and his family held the throne for nearly two centuries,
and art and learning flourished, and magnificent churches
were built, and the borders of the empire steadily expanded.
In the eastern apse of Saint Sophia the subject
of Photios's sermon can still be seen: the Virgin's robe
is a fathomless blue, the archangels' wings exhaust the rainbow.

Braid

In the first portrait
the very small prince is wrapped
in a costume stiff with gold and silver thread.
His dwarf, who is no taller than he
but many years older, appears to lurch
out of the frame, holding the sceptre
and the other symbols of kingship. Later
we see the prince at the riding school.
He is very proud, since he has conquered a horse,
and his entire family watch him from a distant balcony.
He carries a great white plume in his hat,
under the blue and green changes of the Spanish sky.

In the last portrait,
His Highness Prince Baltasar Carlos
appears in hunting costume, a fine cap on his head.
He looks a little puzzled, but none the less resolute,
as he should, since he is heir to a great empire.

The landscape of that empire recedes behind him,
and in it towns are burning, ships are sinking,
and there are buffoons whose eyes are always crossed,
and somewhere an old woman is cooking eggs,
watched by the boy who holds a jar of clear oil.

Miracles occur: a raven descends
with a loaf of bread big enough for two;
lions are digging a saint's grave,
and the young Prince Baltasar Carlos
learns how to ride, learns how to hunt, how
to be a king, and dies in his seventeenth year.
His father must have wept for a day, but then,
for the good of the Hapsburg line, married his son's
betrothed. She, we understand, was sixteen and he
forty-six. This was a small matter of diplomacy.
In the portrait her cheeks are highly rouged.
Her black dress is crossed by many bands of silver braid.

The Ungrateful Citizens

It occurs to me that I would like to write a poem about Naples.
Perhaps I have always wanted to do this, and only realized it just a
    moment ago,
but, alas, I have never been to Naples, and yet my desire to write about
    the place
becomes more insuperable by the second. I become convinced that my
    writing desk
is on the same latitude as Naples: I have only to lean back in my chair,
and I incline toward the city of my dreams, and in my dreams my feet
rest in Manhattan while my hair rustles against the wharves of Naples,
and the wharves are bristling with galleons, feluccas, sloops, and
    schooners,
and how blue the sea on which they sway and jostle, how blue the sky
above them, except for some small clumps of cloud so white they are
    like
roses that have seen ghosts! And one could wander forever in the
    streets

that are as narrow and crooked as the wrinkles on the face of a wise and
 beautiful old woman.
Here all the shop signs are like the titles of arias by Alessandro Scarlatti.
The streets and squares are always busy, yet no one is ever too hurried:
at the slightest opportunity a man or a woman of Naples will sit down
 with you
on some weathered marble doorstep and engage you in the most
 animated conversation
concerning art or politics, your origins, their mother, the latest songs or
 scandals.
A citizen of Naples will say: 'Oh, you are from Brooklyn? I have a
 cousin there.
He tells me it is a very beautiful place.' He will say this out of pure
 courtesy.
In no other city have I seen so many fragrant pots of flowering
 bergamot,
or such luscious leaves of basil, or so many balconies overhung by noble
 bosoms.
In the late afternoon it is customary for the singers to leave the opera
 house,
and go about their business in full costume: here is the Orfeo of
 Monteverdi
haggling over the price of some pomegranates, and over there Dona
 Elvira
is sipping an espresso in a café while sharing a secret with a dishevelled
 Desdemona;
Don Carlos leaves a haberdashers in a fury, while Pinkerton enters a
 tobacconist's,
and Melisande (still in character) weeps beside a baroque public
 fountain
and here is Poppaea, and Dido, and Ariadne, and Judith, and Violetta…
and there goes Madame Butterfly's child eating a fruit like a setting sun
as he saunters down toward the waterfront. There, on the broad
 esplanade,
with its prodigious statuary, many restaurants are to be found,
and they are at once elegant and welcoming. During the heat of the day
their cool marble floors and gently rotating fans are a delight,
and in the evenings entire families go out to dine dressed in the finest
 clothes,
and how charming are the pink and white dresses of the young girls,
who resemble gardenias or oleander flowers as they settle lightly into
 their seats.

The families are very large, which is why the restaurants are so spacious –
stretching away into shimmering distances in which the fans stir the
torpid fronds of palms –
and why the menus are so long and as varied as the colours of autumn.
Here the generations are nightly conjoined in perfect amity,
and even shy lovers may find corners in which to commune unnoticed
except by some musician, who wishes only to urge their love forward
from a tactful distance. The food, it goes without saying, is delicious.
In Naples the taxi drivers have, of necessity, become expert in the
negotiation
of long flights of stairs resembling formalised cascades,
and the buses constantly circling monuments to heroes of the
Risorgimento
seem to be dancing a siciliano as the sunlight rebounds from their
windows
and shatters against the high walls of tenements. Beyond those walls,
however,
in some lightless courtyard a skinny child is crying under lines of
washing
that repeat, day after day, the same doleful sentence, and I am reminded
that this is the city in which songbirds were once blinded so they would
sing
more poignantly in churches on saints' days, beating against the domes
and the vaults...
and it seems that despite the cheerful beggarwomen and roguish
merchants
bowed down by enormous, tufted turbans, despite the bravado
of virile gentlemen dressed like eighteenth-century courtesans that
I had imagined for my Naples,
despite the numberless palaces and paintings, the extravagant churches,
theatres,
and festivals, and the flowers that perfume even the poorest quarters,
it seems that all but the richest and most conservative of citizens cannot
wait to leave my Naples.
They wish to go to the north or far to the west. They crowd the quays
and the airport lounges,
and exhibit the horrible condition of their skin, the rags they are forced
to wear,
the few possessions they drag behind them like so many coffins filled
with stones.
They glare at me and say: 'This is not Naples. This is a place on which
the world has turned its back.

A cloud of lies covers it. The mansions that you saw are hovels, the
    churches tin shacks,
the parks and gardens vegetable plots and stony fields in which we
    scratch for a living.
And this is not even the site of wars and massacres, only a place of
    ordinary wretchedness.
No, we cannot be the amorous ballet the tourist requires for a backdrop –
O take us away, perhaps to the *island of fragrant grasses* mentioned in a
    fragment of Petronius.'

The Drunkard in the Snow

After Trakl

From one age to another,
The little words – the words for darkness,
Or silver, or raw meat,

The offal that is slopped into buckets
At the stark gates where women wait in winter –

From one century to another
At the queasy point of crossing

There is always the stone face of the mother
As her confinement approaches,

The white face of the sister
Like a moon drifting between cold walls –

Always the black brow of the dead town,
And jackdaws above it.

I have seen the father's shadow on the spiral stair,
I have seen him playing with the mirrors of his nightmare.

Always and always…

What has happened is simple as a cube.
Autumn's cymbals clashed
At the hour of my birth. Gutters lay smashed
At the base of blackened walls. My mother's
Hand was cold. Later my sister
Made an unhappy marriage. I no longer
Heard her Schubert sonata in the next room.

O you who were punished for what you did not know,
You who confessed to everything, having nothing to confess,
You simple folk hanging by the neck from the trees,
You know it is not enough, it is never enough
To speak of the blue evenings, the drowned stairs,
And bleeding, bronze heads: they will always excel us.

The poet is always dying
Like a drunkard in the snow,
And the event is a mote in God's eye.

O my young Mathias, my nurse
And attendant (pulled from the mines
To work in the hospital) it was you who wrote:

'Always and always I think about
My dear, good captain. In the evening
He was well, and heartily told me to bring him
Coffee in the morning. But in the morning
It was different, and my captain did not need
Black coffee. Always he protected me. Sir,
I do not wish to be with these people here anymore.'

Twentieth Century

Another bunch of fallen gods returning from the 8th Avenue gym.
The glow of their skin arouses suspicion, could be mere vanity and
    affluence.
They are perhaps creatures from another planet where nocturnes are
    never written?

But they are human under the rind – they read and work – and you
could look a lot more like them if you were prepared to put the time in,
had the stamina to withstand a crushing daily routine, and didn't hate

the very idea of 'exercise'. To what end? To what altar
of sacrifice dedicated? By all means let us return to our drinks and naps
and telephone conversations lest we end up looking like prime beef –

edible no doubt, but hardly food for thought, beyond the most
rudimentary notions and narrations: 'Overcome by the heat,
the handsome electrician hastily undressed, unaware that soon…'

       *

In apartments without curtains, overlooked from many angles,
masturbation is just another of anxiety's inexhaustible wellsprings,
but somehow night no longer answers my desires as once it did,

therefore let all eyelids be raised and a blind sun stand at the zenith.
The voyeur is not the victim of what he sees, and this is no one's
    confession:
I will continue to walk to the left and write with a nose dipped in paint,
    if I so wish –

not that I plan to do anything that would get me arrested,
but most poems, translated to a sunlit street, would be acts of gross
    indecency.
Yes, this is what I've been hiding all these years! It is *your* orphan,
take it in as if it had appeared by moonlight on the steps of a convent.

       *

Some hope! And do not expect anyone to be grateful
for your miraculous aperçu, though some who have followed
the slow progress of your fame may pick it up
like a laundry ticket that has slipped from your pocket

with all the momentousness of Bluebeard's seventh key.
The secret will never be revealed, since there are
no secrets. It is much too late for that. Blood
on the paving stones, blood in the throats of the flowers.

The cleaning fluid is running out. The century is coming to an end,
and to make it look in any way presentable or fit to live in
would be a new labour for Hercules, and yet we *have* lived in it,
and there were days we behaved rationally with nearly stoic calm,

handing out life jackets as the last comforting concept capsized,
and sometimes our clothes, our thoughts, looked elegant and that
    seemed enough:
we had added some feeble lustre to the mostly incriminating record.

             *

A decadent historicism appeared in buildings, appalling to purists,
and executives of telephone companies walked daily
beneath romanesque vaults and the gilded wings of statues,

then on a clouded day no one could fix in retrospect
the body became a religion, sex a kind of makeshift sacrament,
and with nothing but this dim polestar to guide us

we must now confront the idea of continual mourning
and the necessity of pain, as a friend's handsome face
is reduced to something resembling a bruised skull.

It is a time of marvels: in midsummer a wind out of nowhere
strips the trees bare; every few minutes another Marsyas is flayed,
and the same small uncomprehending dog laps at his blood.

Twentieth century, we still have much to learn from you
concerning the refinements of cruelty and its multiplication,
banal as shopping malls on the outskirts of a town,
flourishing as the centre dies and is boarded up.

Twentieth century, you are leaving us
with resurrections of dead gods who remain dead,
twitching in their galvanised graveclothes, and this is unkind,
since we have stayed faithful to you as if you were a good mother.

We ignored your cocaine habit and your masochism –
you appearing in the Irish bar saying, when we mentioned
your face swollen like a purple cabbage: 'Oh I had a bad fall.'

What kind of staircase could do that?
Tell us whose fist it was. Twentieth century, don't lie to us.
We love you and you are leaving forever.